A Guide to Vibrant
Health and Vitality

THE
VIBRANCY
CODES

BY CASSIDY AMBER CHAPMAN

Envealing LLC

Envealing.com

ISBN: 979-8-9868899-0-0

LCCN: Application in Process

CONTENTS

Introduction

I KNOW WHO YOU ARE. YOU ARE THE BEAUTIFUL SOUL
ready to become the embodiment of health, vitality, vibrancy, and deep self-love. You are ready to live a full life
and become truly empowered. You are ready to unlock vibrancy in every area of your life. You may have even been
suffering silently and are ready to implement a solution to
your physical, mental, and emotional pain. Yet, you are not
sure what to do next, and you can't seem to find the answers that you are seeking.

Believe me, I know. I have been there.

This is the book for you. Not only did you pick up the
right book, but you signified to your inner self that you
are ready to figure this out. This moment can be a turning point in your life if you allow it to be. If you are ready
for radical transformation, you are in the right place. Here
you will learn the inner power that you had all along. Once
you finish this book, radical transformation will not only
be revealed to you in steps, but it will become a choice.

Once you implement these methods, your life will become unrecognizable. The codes to unlock vibrancy support you in embodying health at all levels. What does it mean to become vibrant? Merriam-Webster defines *vibrant* as "pulsating with life, vigor or activity[1]." It is the state of being fully alive and connected with life. I discovered that vibrancy is our natural state of being, and once I used these codes, I felt life vibrate within me. I simply allowed it to do so in the present moment. Again, just reading these words does nothing for you. Knowledge is nothing if you don't put it into action. Activating vibrancy is a practice and a result, not a philosophical theory. You do not need to understand how these methodologies work; rather, just feel what they create in your life.

In this book, you will go through the process of listening to the messages from your inner knowing and deeply connecting to your mind, body, emotions, and spirit, which are the first steps to a happy and healthy life. You will understand that no matter where you are, becoming the embodiment of vitality will become inevitable if you choose it. You may be thinking, "Oh god, this woman has got her head in the clouds," and maybe I do, but that is only because of all the miracles I have witnessed and created for myself. No matter who you are, you too can choose the path of receptivity. You can choose to be the embodiment of vibrancy every day. You already have this inside of you. I am just giving you some keys to unlock dormant parts of yourself. The keys to unlock the health, the vitality, and the vibrancy within you. The magic is not only in this book; it is within you

I am writing from my personal experiences and from the experiences of mentoring my clients. I am not claiming to be a doctor, medical professional, therapist, or some type of guru. I am here to help you ignite your innate vibrancy abilities. I am here to show you that you have all the power inside of you. I am here as your guide. You are in the driver's seat. I am here to help turn up the volume on the GPS and turn down all other distractions because the GPS is already telling you which road to take. It is up to you to listen and to take the necessary turns. It is up to you to stay on the road, pay attention to oncoming traffic, and ensure that you are safe on your journey. Make it your own, and know that it is your responsibility to do so.

Before we dive deep, let's cover who this book is not for. This book is not for those seeking just to have embodiment handed to them. A deep, multidimensional, healthy life experience takes time, dedication, and devotion. You are investing in yourself by allowing yourself to transform through reading these powerful words. These codes gifted through these words enact long-lasting life changes that will enable you to live an abundantly healthy life. This book is for the people who genuinely want to create health at all layers.

You may have tried some of these modalities before, but one vibrancy code is not supposed to be the end-all-be-all of your journey or even be a destination at all. You are a multidimensional being that has many parts to you. You have a body, a mind, an emotional body, and a spirit. To find true vibrancy, you must activate vitality at all of these layers. Transformational tools like these have a synergistic nature, which can create miracles. These lifestyle changes can alter your life forever if you are willing to let them.

I will teach you how to embody vibrant physical health, mental health, emotional health, and spiritual health. First, I teach you how to embody physical health by exploring the relationship to your body and using the three D's: Diet, Detox, and Dance. Next, I teach you how to embody mental health by exploring the relationship to the mind and using the three M's: Mind Master, Mind Diet, and Mindfulness. I then teach you how to embody emotional health by surveying your relationship to your emotions and using the three E's: Embrace, Enrich, and

Evolve. I finally teach you how to embody spiritual health by exploring your relationship to spirit and using the three S's: Safety, Surrender, and Serenity. The tools presented here will change your experience of life and hold many of the answers you have been seeking and those you already know. I invite you to feel how the words resonate in your body when something I say speaks truth to you.

However, I will warn you there will be many times in this book that you will feel resistant to what I am inviting you to try, which is a great thing. A breakthrough lies just on the other side of resistance. Nothing will change if you do not do something different. I know this to be true because I still see it every time I embody health more powerfully or evolve a particular area of my life. There is so much resistance until you hit your breakthrough. It is your job to get the fullest value out of this book. There is so much gold here, and some people spend their whole lives getting to the mindset shifts I have presented. Through your commitment to making a change, this will inevitably unfold. I am here to co-create this metamorphosis with you through the immense lessons I have learned.

I will share with you how to tap into your infinite power. How you have always had the chance to be healthy at every level and why starting right now is the perfect time. I am so excited for you to go on this adventure of a lifetime because it can be fun and miraculous all at once. I am so excited for you to transform your health and life. I am thrilled and honored to be your guide. My desire is to lead a beautiful soul like yours to true empowerment because I remember how dark disempowerment can feel. You can learn how to enhance your quality of life through what at first seems like insurmountable odds. When I first started, I was desperate to be heard and have a roadmap to a life worth living. I hear you, see you, and appreciate your willingness to be open to the wisdom in this book and to take action on the embodiment practices I present. This is why I am sharing my story vulnerably, openly, and authentically so that it may empower you to take your health, vitality, and vibrancy into your own hands.

My Vibrancy Story

IT HAS BECOME A RITUAL. I FALL TO MY KNEES AT night with tears streaming down my face, and I thank god with all my heart. I thank the universe because I am alive and for the healing I have been blessed with. I am graced with health, freedom, and courage to live a life free from the shackles of the previous pain I was in. Becoming healthy was one of the best things that ever happened to me, which led to vibrancy, vitality, and a full life beyond what I could have previously imagined. It wasn't always this way. I used to ask for mercy. I would fall to my knees at night, not even knowing what higher power I was talking to. I would just cry, asking God, please hear me, heal me; I can't do this anymore. I felt that my life was no longer worth living and that it was over. Twenty-one-year-old me was ready to throw in the towel. I started struggling with my health at 15 years old with a boatload of symptoms. I gained 50 pounds in under three months eating less than 500 calories per day. I was so nauseous that I couldn't eat. I was dry heaving every day. I had GI pain and dysfunction. I was allergic to over 15 foods. I had painful periods to the point where I would be on the floor crawling to make it to my bed because once my cramps started, I could no longer walk. My PMS was so bad that I would scream-cry for hours. I had recurrent yeast infections that seemed to get more painful every time they came back.

I was so young; I didn't understand what was happening. I started to have many issues that affected my daily living, and I could not figure them out. The doctors I visited told me that my tests came back fine. It was all in my head, or it was just stress or the weight that I had put on. I went to specialist after specialist that performed test after test. My body was telling me something was wrong, but "nothing was wrong with me," according to the tests. This is the first time in medicine that I felt powerless, unheard, unvalued, unseen, and deemed unhelpable. My pain did not feel important to the people I thought were supposed to be my saviors. Many professionals assumed that I was making it up when they couldn't find the answer.

This isn't to say that many professionals I saw didn't try; it is just that they weren't trained to help a girl like me. I was a chronic medical mystery, and getting diagnosed when you have many conflicting symptoms can be very tough. I never fit into one diagnosis box. I ended up having a slew of issues written in my medical file. I always felt defeated when I told others that I was suffering from chronic illness, and they asked about my diagnosis. I felt that I couldn't say one diagnosis because they weren't respected as real diagnoses. Microbiome and autoimmune dysfunctions are not talked about. Sometimes, I still can't find the words to define the pain as I search for validation. I was living with an invisible illness. I now know this is a common problem among diagnoses or illnesses that primarily affect women, and I know that I am not alone.

It took two years of being in and out of doctors' offices with no answers before finding a practitioner who could help me. Finally, my dreams of relief came true when one of the specialists prescribed me a medication that drastically helped with all of my symptoms. For five years, I gratefully took medication that suppressed the problem. All my symptoms came flooding back if I missed a dose, but I didn't care. I just kept making sure I took my medication. I ignored the signs that the illness was ready to come back with a vengeance.

After five years of symptom management, my illnesses had caught up with me. I had a full health crisis because

I had not fully dealt with the root causes. With all of the previous symptoms coming back, I formed new illnesses because my body was tired of keeping up with the other ones. I developed more issues such as chronic urinary tract infections and pelvic pain so painful that it felt like knives were ripping me open from the inside out. I was suffering from severe panic attacks because I was so terrified of the physical pain haunting me. I would either wake up in the middle of the night in severe physical pain or have a full-on panic attack. All I knew was that I was in agony, and I was getting worse day by day.

When my body started to retaliate, I was in absolute unbearable pain. My health crisis was my breaking point. Every night I curled up into the fetal position, praying I would feel some comfort. That effort usually did not help. I would experience even more pain and agony because I was so frustrated that I was in pain and agony. I was so exhausted, but I couldn't sleep due to my distress. I was desperate for rest so that I could have reprieve from my torment. I couldn't handle my affliction anymore; it was too much for me, on top of all the other suffering I was experiencing in my life. I was so sick. I could not get out of bed. I just was done.

I felt powerless and hopeless as no one seemed to be able

to help me. I would go to my doctor's appointments with so much hope to be met with blank and confused faces. I knew their treatment options were only going to make me worse. I felt unseen, unheard, and desperate for answers. My health crisis was not the first time I ever felt this way, but it cut so much deeper when I was in unbearable pain. I remember waking up at three a.m. from a panic attack in severe physical pain. I started to scream into my pillow because my family was asleep. I didn't want to wake them up, as they had stayed up with me too many nights in a row comforting me. I looked up in my pitch-black bedroom as I laid there crying and said, "God please don't let me wake up tomorrow." I was so defeated that I felt that life was no longer worth living because of my pain. My quality of life was completely down the drain, and I couldn't see the end in sight.

During this health crisis, it felt that my entire life was crumbling. Covid hit a few months into my health crisis; the world was breaking with me. Not only was the world in turmoil, but so was my inner circle. I ended a 15-year friendship that had become toxic for both of us, which had felt like a divorce. I had been broken up with by someone I loved deeply, losing a connection that I held close to my heart. The passions that I once had started to slip away as my heart said it was no longer in it. Since I was a child, I have been deeply passionate about being a doctor. However, after being met with blank faces and no answers from so many medical practitioners, my heart was no longer in modern western medicine. I felt that everything I had was gone: my health, what I thought was a lifelong friendship, a relationship I held deeply in my heart, my passion, and my identity. During this one year, I also suffered the death of four family members. I felt that I had died with them even though I was still on earth. My body was in physical pain, my heart was utterly broken, and my soul was shattered.

How did I go from crying for mercy to crying with gratitude? What circumstances allowed me to take charge to change my quality of life? I had a few significant messages come to me that changed my whole world.

One circumstance that pushed me to take back my power was that one of my four family members that died was 32 years old. I knew, once he died, that I had a duty to live my life to the fullest because it all could end so soon.

Life circumstances can be our powerful messages, but so can dreams. I hold dreams in high esteem in my life because they send me messages that are important to me. During this painful period, I had so many nightmares, but there was this one dream that started me on my path.

In this powerful dream, I was walking on the ice of what seemed to be a huge lake of some kind. Through the dark night, I saw miles of ice behind me. In front of me, I saw a hospital about a mile away. The dream was so vivid that I felt the ice on my bare feet, the cold air biting at my skin, parts of my body going numb. It was so dark that I was terrified to move, but I had an inner desperation to get to the hospital. The ice cracked underneath me as I took a step, and I plunged into the ice-cold water. I kept going faster and faster, going deeper and deeper, accelerating through the water until I was miles away from the surface. The moment I stopped going deeper, I looked up and saw just how far from the surface I was. I felt myself give up. I was ready to accept my cold, dark, drowning death. I was ready to have it all end. I was defeated and ready to be taken away.

Suddenly, a will to live swept over me. I looked up and saw there were miles until I could reach the surface. Fear ran through my bones; was it too late to decide to live? I saw a small faint light where I had fallen. I knew I had to try to get there. I started to swim up. There was more and more resistance as I swam, but I didn't let that stop me. I kept swimming and swimming and swimming. It felt like I was swimming for a lifetime until I finally reached the top. I pulled myself out of the water onto the ice. It was the beginning of dawn outside. I celebrated for a moment, but then I realized that I still had no way to get off the ice, and I was all alone. I felt shivering loneliness creep up my spine. I then looked over to the side and saw a boat with two men in it. The boat was half-sunken in the water. The men came over and asked if I needed help, and I said an eager "Yes!" However, I was so confused. In the back of my head, I wondered how they could help me if they were drowning themselves. When I woke up from that dream, I slowly came to three realizations. The first one was that I did not want to die; I wanted to live. The second epiphany I had was that it would be hard to get out of the sunken place I was in. It would take all of my strength, and there would be a lot of resistance. The third understanding that I came to is that I was asking people to help me that were struggling themselves. It was time to become my own savior.

I sat on my bed with my newfound black notebook, and I wrote "Cassidy's Health Plan." I didn't know how I was going to do it, but nothing could stop me. I started doing what I knew best, which was researching. In college, I studied neuroscience which was heavily research-based. I knew how to read research, and I was ready to keep on reading until my eyes bled. I thought my route would be dedicated to resolving my physical ailments, but life had another plan for me. During my journey, I found that I was a multidimensional being that needed to heal at all levels of which I am. To heal at all levels is to be able to see true, deep, and lasting healing. Instead of just looking at my body, I saw myself as mind, body, and soul. Because of the messages I received on my journey, I created my own health action plan, or the first version of it, which guided me to heal physically, mentally, emotionally, and spiritually. I was able to put myself in remission because of my actions and my commitment to getting healthy. I intensely focused on all areas of health, gathering knowledge, strategies, and modalities for self-healing. I gave my body the tools and environment it needed to thrive.

Does this journey to remission mean that it is the end, and I am always fully healthy? The answer is no. It means that I choose embodiment. I choose to practice the keys to health daily. It means that I listen to what my body says and take preventative measures so that I don't go into deep and dark holes of ill health again. Does this healing mean I have no fear about what is to come in my journey of health in the future? No. As I write this book, I still have some fear. I ask myself questions like, "What if I can't keep this up?" and "How long can I sustain this?" This is a natural occurrence of the brain when you achieve something beyond your wildest imagination. Before you achieve this remarkable feat, your mind will tell you it is impossible and then, when you achieve it, that it is impossible to sustain. This mind-chatter is a natural recurrence, and it is ok if your brain can't yet catch up to the beautiful vitality and vibrancy you are creating. There are so many things my brain can't catch up to yet because I went on an accelerated journey where blessings were more than I could comprehend. Is there still fear of pain that I process? Yes, there are times when I fear feeling the immense pain I was in again. However, all this pain has been a gift that I cherish.

I utilized my pain to to fuel the beginning of the most beautiful journey of my life. The journey to my self, my whole self, the healthy vibrant version of myself. I had to painstakingly go through it all and promise myself that I would always be here to save myself. I made very tough decisions, and now I can thank myself. I did it. I saved myself. I am my own hero, my own savior, and my own knight in shining armor. I allowed myself to listen to my inner knowing and ignite my innate healing abilities.

Becoming my own savior and turning on my natural healing processes does not mean that I did not have multiple supports on my journey. Instead, I knew I was worthy of being supported and utilizing resources in the way that served me. I directed my healing path, and I used doctors, medical professionals, and holistic practitioners as tools on my toolbelt. I also found much power in group healing classes, books, courses, and mentorship. I found my first mentor because I was so desperate to fix the relationship I was in. I came across a masterclass about conscious relationships and signed up right away. After attending the masterclass, I was bewildered. I didn't understand some of what the instructor was talking about. I then signed up for a conscious relationship course, and I did not start mentorship until after my breakup. At first, I signed up because I wanted the relationship to be put back together. However, that is when my mentor showed me that it was the relationship with myself that I needed to put back together, leading me down a beautiful path of self-healing, self-belief, vibrancy activation, and a journey I hold dear to my heart.

Through every opportunity I had, I took back my power. Now, I feel liberated. Life is in my control. I am the driver instead of the passenger. I can wield my healing power throughout my entire life. I will use each tool in my toolbox to continue to embody health every day, week, month, and year. I am dedicated every day to living vibrantly. I am so grateful for choosing this journey because otherwise, I would not be writing to you. I am here to help. You are not alone in your journey. People who have truly become successful in something want others to join them. I want you to join me and bask in the light of this everlasting vibrancy.

You may be thinking, "I am not sure if this holistic thing is for me." I felt that way, too, but something deep inside of me told me that it was something that I desperately needed to try. I would get so angry when other people would tell me that my pain was emotional. I would tell them that they were not acknowledging that I was suffering. It took me a long time to recognize that I needed to be the one to acknowledge my torment. I had nothing to prove or defend to anyone. My struggles were real, and I was going to get myself a better quality of life. I needed to choose to save myself. Some of the methods I tried seemed woo-woo at first, and then they started to work and completely changed my perspective. I began to see the world differently. I began to see and feel magic. I was like a kid again, and the world was full of wonder, waking me back up into enchantment. I have realized throughout this journey that we can have any perspective we want because we choose it. Isn't it way more fun to believe in magic?

I chose to live in this magical playground, and I will not go back. I love being in a world full of wonder and possibilities. It is so funny how when you start to see the infinite possibilities, they become real. I feel safe knowing that I can create any reality I wish. I now remember we are infinite beings capable of anything. I am so excited for you to explore and discover your own beliefs that serve you.

I went from not being able to get out of bed to jumping out of bed in the morning so excited that I have been gifted a new day. That first moment I wake up, I sip in the elixir of life with my first conscious deep breath.

I was in a deep and dark place, but I got out. Even against what seems like insurmountable odds, make an intention and act on that intention every single day.

My vibrancy is my most treasured gift. True multidimensional health, vitality, and vibrancy is not a destination; it is a journey. I have a burning desire to give back this vibrancy because I have been so blessed to have this newfound full life. I am here for you. I want you to have the transformation I have had and continue to experience. However, only you can commit to this journey. Are you ready?

EMBODIMENT PRACTICE

Knowledge is nothing without implementation. Throughout this book, I will provide you with embodiment practices to try now. Your attempt doesn't have to be pretty or perfect. The real power comes from you showing up and the energy you give. Just show up and try. I know it isn't always easy, but that is why the reward of just sitting down to do these practices will be so grand.

Dream Journaling:

I invite you to keep a dream journal even if you do not always remember your dreams or have yet to remember them. Keep a journal on your bedside table ready for you when you first wake up. Just by having the intention to remember your dreams, you are extremely more likely to do so. It is important that you know what your subconscious is trying to tell you or what it is processing. Keeping a dream journal allows you to remember. When you wake up, try to remember your dream and write it down. Sit with what you think it means. I bet you that you will understand it just by taking the time to sit down and try. When you start asking powerful questions, powerful answers show up. What is this dream telling me? What does my subconscious want me to know? Ask these questions to yourself and write down the first thing that comes to mind, even if you are unsure. Also, dreams can have multiple meanings. It is all about listening to the profound messages in them and taking the time to do so

PART I
Embodying Vibrant Physical Health

THE POWER
OF THE BODY

YOUR BODY WORKS IN COMPLEX AND MAGNIFICENT ways. Every single inch of your being is alive. You have infinite capabilities, and you use this power effortlessly. It has become normalized to take your magnificent vehicle of life for granted, yet they do so much for you.

You do not have to be consciously aware that you are breathing or that your heart is continuously beating. The average adult has around 20,000 breaths a day, with each breath being a gift[2]. The average heart beats around 60 to 100 beats per minute or over 48 million times per year[3] . Each of your cells contains the same DNA yet can be expressed in infinite ways, creating the individual that is you[4].

You can even turn genes on and off based on what you do in your environment. This procedure is called epigenetics[5]. This majestic process allows you a chance to overcome even your genetic code, giving you the power to take back your health if you so choose[6]. You can change and morph the expression of your DNA based on things you think, say, and do.

The brain is the organ that we most often take for granted. It is the control center of how we think and act, based on electrical and chemical signaling. The process of how your brain, the most captivating organ, works is quite simple. Ions like sodium and potassium come in and out of a cell to produce an electrical current which then releases a chemical to tell another neuron to produce an electrical current, and this process is repeated. That is it. Every thought, every action, and every command your brain gives to your body is done through these simple mechanisms. Each of your neurons has an endless capacity to provide you with what to say, think, and do[7].

Each neuron does not have its own identity because they have immeasurable possibilities. Your neurons tell you how to do everything. They help you brush your teeth, solve math problems, fall in love, and so much more. Each neuron has infinite phenomenal possibilities. You can even change your brain structure by what you do. In just a few weeks or months, your actions may create new neural connections, make a part of your brain denser, or generate more function in a brain area than before[8].

Your ability to heal yourself is incredible, and many times you are most likely taking this gift for granted. You are an endless being, and each one of your cells is a representation of that. Stem cells can be turned into any other cell in your body. You still can naturally produce stem cells now; these cells are not limited to infant development[9]. You can produce unlimited possibilities without even being aware that you are doing it. It is an effortless act of your systems.

Your body is so impressive that it is easy to forget to be grateful for it; you may just assume it will stay maintained. When you get sick or feel pain, you can think your body is against you, but it is absolutely not. Your incredible systems constantly keep you maintained so you can live a happy, healthy, and vibrant life. Pains and illness are ways to wake you up and tell you to make a change. These pains can also be a sign that you need to rest to accomplish some healing.

There is no evidence that the body is against you. In some severe cases, you may say, "I have an autoimmune disease. My cells are literally attacking me." Your immune system isn't attacking you on purpose. It is trying to save you from invaders; it just is having a hard time seeing which cells are harmful. As you give your immune system more tools, it can start to learn what your own cells are.

The human body learns so fast because it is trying to keep you alive with all of its strength. Even in the case of cancer, your cell production centers are doing their best to give you the cells you need to function. Your cell's regulators just don't recognize that it is making too much. Your capillaries supply blood to these cancer cells because it thinks it is nurturing you. I am not saying these are pleasant experiences; rather, they are some extremely traumatic experiences. However, being against your body and being angry at your body will not be conducive to healing it. Every system, organ, and cell you have is doing everything it can to make you thrive. That is the biological wiring. Your body is better than a best friend because it looks after you 24/7, trying to make things right for you.

Did you know that if the DNA inside you was uncoiled, it could wrap around the earth about 2.5 million times[10]? Your body can condense this much information into microscopic cells with room for other organelles, ions, and functions. You are way more than you give yourself credit for, and you are more capable than you can even comprehend. You do not have abundance; you truly are abundance. Your systems, organs, bones, tissues, and cells are magnificent; each deserves your thanks and keen attention.

You are a universe in yourself. Your systems are your galaxies, like your digestive, respiratory, and detoxification systems. Your organs are the different planets, like the heart, brain, and liver. Your cells are the inhabitants of the planets; they are the life form. These components work together to create a beautiful universe that is you.

Our bodies talk to us through pain and illness; they are like prayers. Your body is praying to you, asking your grace for attention, affection, and assistance. Your body is saying, "Hear me so that you can heal me." This is your body's cry for help. Now let's learn how to listen and how to answer these calls. It is all about giving your body the tools and environment it needs to thrive and believing that you can do it. Are you going to listen to your body? Are you going to provide it with the tools it needs to thrive and utilize your innate healing power?

Most people know what they need to do for their physical health but rarely do they actually do it. They are disconnected from their bodies and the messages they send. Most people think it is normal to be bloated, crampy, and have digestive issues. However, this is not normal; our society has just normalized it based on the number of people experiencing it. It is common knowledge most of the time to eat well, exercise, etc., but few know the sheer importance of making small choices daily that put you towards health. It is vital to take every step towards vitality because health affects every area of your life. These codes are about consistent small action. You create a deeply loving and grateful relationship with your body and create habits to express that love. I will review what I call the three D's: Diet, Detox, and Dance—the three main vibrancy codes of embodying physical health—and explain how I used messages from my body to cultivate my new lifestyle.

EMBODIMENT PRACTICE

Connecting to your body:

1. Sit down and first thank your body and tell your body that you love it.

2. Ask your body, "How are you feeling?"

3. Ask if it needs anything.

4. Sit down and do a body scan. Put your awareness first at the top of your head, to your face, neck, shoulders, down your arms to your fingertips. Use your awareness to scan down your chest and stomach. In the torso, check if anything feels off where

each of your organs are. Make sure to check your back how is your back feeling, then scan your hips, your legs, all the way to the tips of your toes. Notice if you feel any heaviness or tension.

5. Ask your body again if it needs anything.

6. If you get an answer, give your body what it needs.

7. If you don't get an answer but still would like to give your body a gift, then do what you want to do for your body and say, "This is an act of devotion to you, I am grateful for all that you do for me, and I desire to do this for you."

8. Repeat this process multiple times a day to become truly connected to your body.

CHAPTER 1

Diet

Using Intuition to Guide Food Choices

THERE ARE SO MANY MISCONCEPTIONS ABOUT WHAT A diet is, but it truly is an accumulation of habits around items that you consume, i.e., food, beverages, supplements, and herbs. It is very easy to get frustrated with diet. Our society is bombarded with diets that are either not beneficial or do not create long-lasting changes. We are instinctual beings and can intuitively know what our body needs to consume. Diet culture has been messing with our heads for too long, and it is important to know the difference between diet and detox. A diet is defined as long-term habits around food, not that month you went on a smoothie cleanse. That is a detox, which is short-term.

At first, you may get frustrated with your diet because you failed to see "results." You may think that eliminating a certain food or adding a different type of food was supposed to help and you then feel defeated when you did not see the results you were looking for (i.e., relief of pain, relief of illness, or loss of weight). This approach does not serve you and your health. Instead, take the approach of creating long-term changes. This is when you cultivate a real connection to your body. Failing to see any results can be exhausting; however, visible results are not the goal. The real goal is to provide your body with the tools and environment to thrive. The goal is to connect to your body to know what nourishes you and what is hard for you to process. No matter what lifestyle you follow, it is always best to cut out as much processed food as possible and opt for whole foods. There are so many diets out there, but it is up to you to decide what lifestyle changes work best for you.

Every diet will look different for each personal health journey. We can use food as medicine, but how exactly do we do that? Well, you want to use your intuition and resources that are suitable for your specific needs. You want to use your instincts and messages from your body to figure out which foods are best for you

Messages from our inner knowing can be clear and profound, especially in dreams. One night I had a dream that was such a clear message to me as I woke up. In this dream, I was in this mental institution, and I was surrounded by a whole bunch of characters from Sesame Street, Disney, etc. I saw Elmo in a wheelchair and Big Bird on a bed with oxygen being supplied to him. I realized that I was a pink and purple dragon, not like Barnie but more of a fluorescent and majestic one that I had not seen before. As I looked around, every one of the characters looked like they were being drugged. They all had IVs attached to them and were slumped down. I could see that none of them were functioning; they could barely stay awake, let alone walk. None of them seemed to be aware that they were being drugged, or maybe they just didn't care.

I was taken into a room with a hospital bed, and the nurse put in an IV drip. The bag said, "IV sugar." Immediately, I felt the effects of cloudiness and was unable to move my body. I kept trying to move, but my body felt glued to the hospital bed and this prison of IV sugar. I felt as if I was heavily drugged. I did not want to let someone poison me; that wasn't the life I wanted to live. I felt a calling to be free. When the nurses weren't watching, I ripped the IV out. I barely got out of the bed, using my remaining strength to crawl to the exit. As I passed the hospital exit, I looked behind me and saw the nurses running toward me, screaming to capture me. I remembered at that moment that I had wings and it was time to start using them. As the doors opened once again, I used all of my strength to open up my wings and attempt to fly. My first try was not successful; it seemed it had been a long time since I was able to fly. As soon as someone grabbed my leg to pull me back into this prison, I got the groove of using my wings. As I flew away, I noticed my pink and purple colors become more fluorescent, which is when I woke up. As I sat up in my bed, I realized that sugar was addictive, a drug, keeping me from being free.

Sometimes your intuition is hard to hear when it comes to food choices because we can get clouded by sugar. Not the sugar in fruit or natural sources, but refined sugar. The reason that sugar clouds your intuition is that it is addictive. In a study done by Serge H Ahmed, researchers found through animal studies that sugar is just as addictive as cocaine or may even surpass the addictive quality[11]. Persistent sugar cravings can cloud the gut feeling in your stomach that tells you what is and isn't good for you. My own experience illuminated this idea to me. I found that cutting out refined sugar from my diet was hard at first because of the cravings, but I no longer craved it after a while. Instead,

I started to be a little repulsed by it because I was listening to my body, which told me that sugar was not good for me. Once I cut out refined sugar, I also noticed that everything started to taste so much better. Some foods and beverages that I didn't think were sweet before became my sweet foods. Your brain rewires itself when you allow it the chance to get over the addiction and listen to what your body truly wants.

After I cut out sugar, I started to realize the sheer amount of sugar the food industry exploits because of its addictive qualities. I was shocked when I noticed how often sugar was added to food, because refined sugar has absolutely no nutritional value[12]. This realization pushed me towards whole foods. I ate as many fruits, vegetables, and other non-processed foods as possible. My system became so much clearer. Fruits became my dessert and vegetables the main part of my meal. Whatever will get you into a better place than you are right now is a step in the right direction. It takes baby steps to make lasting changes and experience results.

You can see from my dream that I received the message that sugar was dangerous to my health, but this does not mean that the same holds true for you. You do not immediately have to stop eating sugar or even stop eating it at all. I do not subscribe to the idea that there is one miracle diet, but I do believe in listening to what your body is asking for. All I am asking you to do is listen to your own body and the messages you receive. What works for one person will not work for all. If you feel anger rising while you read this section or feel defeated, believe me, I understand. I was in your shoes, and I remember the difficulty of making such decisions. It wasn't until I was in the ultimate crisis and unbearable pain that I made the switch to truly listen to my body. A combination of multidimensional tools will ignite your natural healing abilities; you just have to commit to finding them. It all starts with committing to yourself.

Another obstacle that stands in the way of people looking to change their diet is the feeling of limitation. I used to feel limited by my food choices because I had to cut out so much that I was eating. Then I realized that I had the absolute privilege of choosing my food. I had the privilege to have access to fruits, vegetables, and non-processed foods. I had the privilege to nourish my body with the foods it was asking for. Once I started seeing the abundance of healthy food, a whole new world opened up to me. I explored different ways of cooking delicious, healthy food. It became a fun game and enhanced the quality of my life. A mindset shift is vital to creating a loving relationship with food.

Your relationship with food is essential in creating a diet that supports health, vibrancy, and vitality. I remember how bad my relationship was with food. I had over 15 allergies to foods. However, I wanted to stay silent about them because I was utterly embarrassed that I had them in the first place. It felt like a dirty secret that separated me from humanity. I also was taught in my family that food is a way to share and express love. I wasn't able to accept that type of expression of love from others because of my "limitations." When I went to gatherings, I would be so embarrassed that I couldn't have the food there, so I would just say "I am not hungry" because I was afraid I was going to get sick and too embarrassed to say I had allergies. This made people sad because they thought I just didn't want to eat their food. I was afraid even to ask what the ingredients were because someone would ask why and then ask if I had an allergy. It never made sense to me to say every allergy I had because there were over 15 of them. I would just take my chances when I was extremely hungry and had such fear that I would get sick, even when the meal was something I could eat, my body wouldn't process it well because I was eating in a state of fear.

When I first started gaining a lot of weight, it wasn't

from the amount of food I was eating. It was because of my microbiome, which I didn't understand at the time, and which I will further explain in the section on detox. I was eating less than 500 calories per day and still gaining over 50 pounds in under three months. After my rapid weight gain, I would experiment to see how my body would react to different amounts of food. I could eat under 500 calories per day for weeks, or over 2000 calories per day for weeks, and I would still gain weight or look and feel heavier. This confused me so much and deeply affected my relationship with food. I also was accused of closet eating when I first started to gain weight because, in other people's reality, it wasn't possible to gain that amount of weight with that amount of calories. These comments made me so angry at my body and myself. They made me question my calculations because I started to write down everything I was eating and how much to prove how little it was and that my appetite was off. Feeling like I had to constantly prove I was sick was instrumental in keeping me sick. I felt that it didn't matter what I was eating, so I came from a place of eating just to eat and that what I ate didn't matter. Now, this isn't to say I didn't eat moderately healthy; I did. I had not eaten any fast food since I was seven years old, I had a good amount of vegetables in my diet, and I felt that I was eating healthier than most people because I was allergic to lots of processed food. I also felt as though I was against food. I would be so mad at food if I got sick and mad at my body for getting sick from the food. I was angry at my situation in general, and I resisted the reality I was living in. Through so much resistance, I was constantly bloated, and my stomach pretty much always hurt, so much so that the pain became normal to me.

Changing my relationship with food required surrendering to my circumstances. When I started to be deeply connected to my body, I learned what it wanted to eat. I loved my body enough to nourish it with the nutrients it desired. I gave my body the tools it needed to be the vessel of my dreams and desires. When I learned that my body is what comes with me into my future, I realized it needed my keen attention and thanks. When I started to have deep gratitude for my body, I no longer felt sick as I was eating because I was listening to what my body did and did not want.

I cultivated a deep love for my body, where I am in awe of its healing capabilities and its love for me. I also gave myself permission to be conscious about what I put in my body and know that it matters. I am allowed to be conscious about what is in my food; I am allowed to be open about what I choose to put in my body and what I don't and be unapologetic about it. As I started to become vocal about my food choices, I realized that I became a mirror for others' insecurities when it came to food. Eating to nourish myself and loving my body triggers many people around me because it brings up their own relationship with food. It is important to be unapologetic about the healthy habits that you create for yourself.

When I became unapologetic around food, my intentions while eating changed, creating a beautiful experience that I love immersing myself in daily. I created such a loving relationship with my body, that it responded with many gifts. Because I was listening to my body, nourishing it, and staying away from foods it did not want to break down, I was no longer allergic to 12 of those 15 foods I was originally allergic to. Surrendering to my reality allowed me to create a new one.

Your relationship with food can change how you absorb nutrients or break them down. Your intentions when eating are crucial in making sure that you are listening to your body. Do you blame yourself every time you try to pick up food? Are you honoring your body as you eat? Are you in an anxious state while eating, or are you joyful while eating? If you feel that you are eating "bad" food, then that intention will cause your body to feel that the food you are eating is dangerous.

Your body is listening to you, and being in a state of joy while eating food can radically change your relationship with food and your body. A mindset shift that can help you make food choices that serve you is approaching eating with the mantra, "I am here to nourish my body," or "I am giving my body the tools so that it can lovingly bring me into health."

When we think of diet, we should be looking at giving our bodies the nourishment and tools they need to thrive. Sometimes we have deficiencies, or our body needs extra tools such as supplements to get to a healthy state. Supplements are fantastic when used correctly and with the right mindset. It is dangerous to use supplements with the medication mindset, where you believe one supplement will completely heal your body. You will be highly disappointed and defeated if you expect one tool, one diet, one supplement to be all that you need to completely heal. The goal here is not to rely on a pill that suppresses your symptoms but rather to aid your body in healing. Supplements, and all of these modalities, are meant to be combined with others.

Supplements can be a powerful tool in your journey to embodying health. They are in mine. Use your intuition as much as possible when it comes to taking supplements because your body knows what it needs; you just have to listen. I have become extremely connected to my body, and I understand what supplements my body needs. However, if you are not yet at this stage of complete connection with your body, you may want to use assistance in figuring out which supplements may help you. You may need multiple tests to see how to incorporate supplements into your diet. If you go to your doctor or functional medicine practitioner and ask for a panel on the vitamins and minerals in your blood, they will make sure that you have no deficiencies that may be causing underlying issues.

The food you eat can also cause underlying issues that create pain and illness. If your body is telling you that a certain food is not good for you, then it is a good idea to stay away from it. I have seen many people ignore food sensitivities and subtle allergies. This can be highly disruptive to your system. If your body constantly has to use its precious resources to break down food that it does not want, it takes away energy from other vital processes that keep you in health. Again, if you are not yet highly connected to your body and its wants and needs, you may want to find assistance in figuring out which foods to eat and which to stay away from. Food allergies and sensitivities can be tricky because we are told that if you are not anaphylactic to a food, you are not allergic. Your body can still create histamines against food that it thinks is an invader and experience a wide range of reactions. Food allergies can cause underlying issues and contribute to inflammation. Eliminating these foods could be a huge key to becoming vibrantly healthy.

It is solely up to you what you want to consume. Always ask how your body feels after consuming different foods. This is your experiment to see what works for you and learn to listen to your intuition. Sometimes just asking the question of how your body feels after you eat can get you more connected to your food intuition.

What lifelong changes are you ready to commit to? What baby step are you going to start today? What foods are in your highest good? Are you willing to start listening to what your body is asking for and what it wants to stay away from?

EMBODIMENT PRACTICE

Figuring out the foods that nourish you:

1. Sit down and listen to your body after eating different types of food.

2. Start to write down the ones that make your body feel the best. (When I say best, I do not mean the dopamine hit you get from eating but how your body feels while processing it.)

3. Start to write down the ones that do not make you feel great.

4. Then plan to start to eat more of those foods that make your body feel good.

5. Also start to notice the times of the day that your body seems to like that particular food.

6. It is so imperative to take the time to sit and listen to your body.

CHAPTER 2

Detox
Releasing Physical Toxins

IN OUR SOCIETY, WE HAVE PUT OUR BODIES IN TOXIC overload, creating a great need to detox, which is the process of allowing your body to cleanse out the stuck toxins or giving your body a break from adding more toxins. Getting rid of stored toxins allows your systems to restore you to health. We are bombarded with marketers trying to get us to use a plethora of products, but they truly are not thinking about our health. These marketers are not bad people; they are making products that last and are cost-effective. It is important to look at the ingredients and be cognizant of their effects on you.

Before we go over the different ways to detox, it should be noted that one method will not be the end all be all of your health journey. You will have to try many strategies, and you will be frustrated if you expect one part of your plan to make you vibrantly holistically healthy. As you get into action, you find the right combination of healing modalities that ignite your innate healing abilities.

First and foremost, the healthiest and most universal detox innate within us is utilizing the power of water. As a society, we do not drink enough water because there are so many other drinks out there for us to consume on a regular basis, like coffee, soda, alcohol, juice, and energy drinks. I realized when helping a client that she seemed to be surprised by what I said about the importance of water and that this tool needed to be explicitly spoken about. To me, drinking water becomes more effortless because I stay away from sugar, which is pretty much what other drinks besides water are made of. By listening to my body, I know when I need water before I get thirsty. If you get thirsty, you are likely extremely dehydrated. You might read this statement and ask, "huh?" When we first get dehydrated, we get hungry before we get thirsty. This phenomenon contributes to some people's snacky periods, where they can't seem to get satisfied when eating. It doesn't always mean they are hungry. It can mean that they are thirsty. By eating those snacks, they are probably making themselves even more thirsty. Our bodies learned to get hungry before thirsty because there was usually not a water source near us in the time of hunting and gathering. We would get hungry so that we could eat a fruit or vegetable, which has high water content. However, most of the time, when you are grabbing a snack, you are not grabbing a fruit or a vegetable and are most likely picking a snack with no water content, hence why you are not satisfied. Our bodies first seek water through food[13].

Water is imperative to your body's ability to detox. Water is one of the most versatile and powerful elements that can flush out anything not serving your body. With all of these detox methods, it is important to remember to drink lots of water. When I say "drink lots of water," there is one health and safety tip I will note here: you can actually drink too much water if it isn't the right kind. The truth is, we can hurt ourselves by drinking too much water. You may ask, "Then why are you telling me to drink more water?!" Well, there is a second reason our bodies seek fruits or vegetables instead of water. It is because we need water to have electrolytes in it as well. If you drink too much water without electrolytes at once, you can change the balance of ions in your body, which can be extremely dangerous[14].

I made the mistake of drinking too much nonelectrolyte water once, which was scary. I could feel my hands and feet start to tingle as vertigo spread throughout my body. I could tell something was off. It happened quickly after a period of chugging water. This was when I learned I needed electrolytes in drinks, and when my confusion set in. Why doesn't everyone know this? Why isn't this common knowledge? Well, you probably will not get to the point of drinking too much water that you throw your ions off balance because you need to drink a ridiculous amount of water at one time to do that. However, I experienced it because I was trying to abuse the benefits of water when I was extremely sick, instead of listening to what else my body needed and trusting that my body could heal. I was trying to use water with the medication mindset. This mindset in itself is dangerous. So, as you start drinking more water, remember that some of those drinks should include electrolytes. Now, I do not mean the super sugary electrolyte drinks you see in sports advertisements. I mean regular water with added electrolytes. There are plenty of recipes that will help you add electrolytes yourself. Another healthy alternative is coconut water, which naturally has plenty of electrolytes. Drinking water is a natural and effortless way to detox and something you can act on right now.

Another way to detox naturally is intermittent fasting, which can last a range of different times. I use fasting for around 15 to 16 hours, the break between my last meal of the day and the first meal the next day. If you try this fast, you spend most of that time sleeping, making this method much easier than other fasts. There is much controversy around this subject, as it seems scientists are trying to say whether it is suitable for everyone. There may be a significantly dangerous difference for women who practice intermittent fasting for too long. Recognizing that this is a detox and not a diet may help bridge the gap. Some may abuse this tool and make it a diet instead of utilizing it to heal the body. It is about giving your body a break, not about starving oneself. Consider intermittent fasting if your body is asking for a break and needs a detox. Of course, we all need different styles of eating and food choices as we listen to our bodies. If you naturally are not hungry one morning but are forcing yourself to eat breakfast, or if you are just in the habit of eating breakfast and are not hungry, this could be a great detox for you for that day. Becoming more conscious of when your body is hungry also allows you to bring in more intuitive eating. Eat when your body wants to be nourished and not because you have time. If this method feels right to you, go ahead and try it. If it doesn't, honor your choice for yourself. I am telling you about this method because of the amazing benefits I have seen in my life.

One more active way to detox is by going to a sauna. Usually, your local gym will have one of these or some other facility close by you. Saunas have a wide variety of health benefits besides just sweating out the toxins from your body. They have been shown to reduce the frequency of colds[15], boost cardiac function[16], reduce symptoms in those with chronic inflammation illnesses, and help purify your system[17]. Saunas are also a great way to relax, so win-win. While researching for this book, I realized there are many benefits to saunas, yet I had never tried one because I was too scared. While writing this chapter, I had gotten tonsilitis while I was away in a foreign country in an apartment with a sauna in it. While I was sick, I asked my body if it was something it wanted to experience, and I got a clear yes. The sauna immediately helped with how I was feeling, and I recovered much faster than I expected. I started using it every day after that for the rest of the month. I kept doing it because it made my body feel so good. Sauna sessions are not for everyone or for every moment, so listen to your intuition. Is your body calling for a sauna?

Foot detox baths, also known as ionic foot baths, were

another significant part of my journey. To serve as a warning, you might feel worse as I did during my first detox bath because I didn't replenish my minerals afterward. If you go and get an ionic foot bath, then make sure to bring mineral water of some sort. That also goes for any of the other detoxes; make sure to stay hydrated and that you are getting the correct minerals. You also want to eat clean foods afterward because it is important to support yourself through these processes.

Additionally, there is the elimination detox. Elimination detox is when you eliminate foods that can be triggering inflammation for a week to three weeks. The most common foods that people eliminate during this time are dairy, gluten, refined sugar, fried foods, and overly processed foods. These eliminations usually include staying away from alcohol and any unnecessary drugs. Eliminating these foods for an acute period can aid your body in regulating without having to break down food too much. You want to fuel your body with nutrients instead of burdening it with having to break down complex foods and substances when it should spend that time repairing your body and bringing it to homeostasis.

Detoxing is essential to your healing process as it allows your body to have room to do what it needs. A juice or smoothie cleanse is a great way to reset your system because all you digest is liquids. It isn't about losing weight per se but just know that it is a possibility, and please do not try to come into a detox with the need to lose weight. First, it isn't sustainable weight loss. Second, it can be dangerous to have this mindset during a detox because it becomes about being a disservice to your body (trying to starve it) instead of being in devotion to your body. Detoxes are about giving your body a break so that they can help you stay in homeostasis. Again, recognize that there is a difference between diet and detox and that this is a detox. These smoothie or juice cleanses are usually utilized with the diet culture mentality which, does not serve your body. Using this method to be for your body and not against it is crucial. You can utilize this detox for about 24 hours to five days. The duration period is all up to you; listen to what your body tells you. The body's systems start to crash when it isn't able to clear itself because of excess stored toxins. When bodies are overloaded, it is the same as a fish trying to swim upstream. Detoxes can provide huge improvements on a health journey when used wisely because they allow more room for vitality to vibrate in the body.

Detoxes are also extremely important because they help create a healthy microbiome and reduce inflammation.

What is the microbiome? It is the bacteria that live in your body, and where people focus on it the most is in the gut. We have 100 trillion of these bacteria throughout our bodies. These bacteria regulate almost everything, from how food is broken down, to mental health status, to the functionality of the immune system[18], to the development of chronic inflammatory diseases, to weight management[19]. A case study by the Infectious Disease Society of America found that after a woman was treated for a condition with fecal matter, a treatment that can help with microbiome dysfunction, she quickly gained significant amounts of weight without changing the amount of food or the type of food she was eating. Why did this woman gain so much weight so fast? The stool donor was obese, and her microbiome looks to have contributed to the smaller woman's rapid weight gain[20]. Our bacteria have a huge role in our weight and our everyday lives. Just by working on healing my microbiome, I lost over 60 pounds, and now I realize why I gained weight so fast while eating a little amount.

The reason so many of us have to clean our guts is that we have become a society reliant on antibiotics. We overuse them, which in turn destroys our microbiome. Now, this isn't to say antibiotics aren't great medical marvels. It is just that we use them too much, and that shouldn't be our first line of defense. Through my research, I learned that my microbiome was deeply affected when I had major surgery when I was ten which had me on antibiotics for an entire year. Now I think no wonder my health started to go sideways for so long; my microbiome had been severely damaged. In a Ted Talk, Rob Knight mentions this concept and talks about how taking antibiotics once might harm our microbiome for years[21].

We must replenish our microbiome because it is incredible what the microbiome is for us and what it does. You can try to replenish the microbiome by taking probiotics or eating fermented foods (naturally created probiotics), which have also been shown to reduce gut inflammation. Some people eat fermented foods like kimchi and kombucha to get their microbiome back. You might need to be careful because these are high histamine foods which are not great for everyone; listen to your body's needs and wants. Whether they naturally occur or not, these probiotics, taken with prebiotic fiber, aid your body in getting even more benefits from the probiotics. Another way to replenish your microbiome is by reducing sugar intake because sugar itself can disrupt the bacterial balance[22]. You can also get a better microbiome through something called grounding. This is when your bare feet are on grass. This helps you possibly because of the earth's microbiome[23] and because your electricity balances out. We are electric beings, and the earth grounds us, just as the electricity in our home needs to be grounded[24].

Your gut produces 95 percent of the serotonin in your body. Serotonin is the neurotransmitter that is associated with depression when levels are low[25]. What we eat has such a huge impact because it can either nourish or disrupt our vast and complex systems. Your microbiome also changes based on your diet. If you "heal your gut," many great things can happen for you. Another fascinating fact is that our microbiome loves when we do intermediate fasting. Since bacteria helps us break down food, it needs breaks to use its energy towards other important aspects of growing and regulating our systems[26]. The goal is to provide your body with the tools and environments for you to not only survive but thrive. Detoxing is imperative to our microbiome system, which in turn brings us many benefits.

We are in a state of survival most of the time because our toxic load is so high. One way to get the real benefits of detox is by lowering your toxic load. There are so many ingredients in our daily products that we do not usually think about, but that have real implications on our health.

This is when you look at your shampoos, toothpaste, laundry detergent, dishwashing liquid, makeup, etc. These create massive shifts in your toxic overload. I could write an entire book on the different ingredients in these products and how they have real implications on the body. A way to imagine this is to think of your skin as your body's biggest organ. Does that change the way you automatically put something on it? Each company says their products are safe because they contain only a little (or a minuscule amount) of toxic ingredients, but they are not thinking about the multiplier effect. When you have something in your body that is a little toxic and then another toxin, the effects on your body multiply[27]. If your body is trying to get rid of the toxins in your toothpaste and your laundry detergent, when will it have time to bring you back to balance or bring you to deeper levels of health? By getting everything that you can as clean as possible, you are making decisions towards health in every aspect of your life.

One of the most common toxins we add into our bodies as adults is alcohol so let's talk about it. For many years, I did not give up this substance. Red wine, in particular, can have many health benefits, and oh, how I loved wine. I even called myself a wino or blamed it on the fact that because I was Italian, it was in my blood. I saw drinking as a part of my identity. My body, however, was telling me that alcohol was no longer meant to be anywhere near my body. I had a slight existential crisis when I realized that my body was asking me to stop drinking alcohol. Maybe it had been for years, but I never stopped to listen. I only stopped drinking because my body was screaming this time instead of its usual whisper. At first, I said I was taking a break from alcohol. My friends and family waited for me to start to drink again. Then I felt this immense pressure to start drinking again because I had attached it to my identity for so long, and I did not want to be an outsider. The more I was connected to my body, the more I realized it did not want alcohol. I had to let go of the identity of the girl who drank for the girl who listened to her body. It is not easy to tell your friends and family this is a choice you are making because it can make you feel like an outsider. However, the more I don't drink, the more I realize there are others around who don't drink as well and that it doesn't matter.

I am not saying that I will never drink alcohol again. Maybe that is the case. All I know is I listen to my body and spirit intently. If my soul feels that I am supposed to experience a night where I drink, I will listen. However, until that day comes, I will stay true to my own being first and foremost. I am not going to tell you to give up alcohol forever or tell you to give it up at all. I am just going to ask you a couple of questions. Do you feel sick almost immediately after drinking just a little bit of alcohol? Does your body feel that it cannot process it? Are you actually enjoying it, or is it just because you are in an environment where drinking is encouraged? What is your intention when drinking? If you feel amazing while drinking, afterward, and the next day, do whatever makes your body feel good. Even if you know you will not feel good, allow yourself to have a conscious intention of the consequences. What one person's body tells them may be different from the next. I cannot say this enough: sit with your body ask it questions and listen to your body's responses because it will tell you what it wants and doesn't want.

When you first become super connected to your body, you may feel uncomfortable at first. You may experience a healing crisis—this especially happens with detoxes. It looks different in everyone, but essentially it is when you feel worse before you start to feel better. Do not be discouraged by this statement, and again realize that sometimes your pain is a result of your body doing what it needs to do so that you can be healthy and live in homeostasis (the term used when your body is completely in balance).

For example, the healing crises I went through went a

little something like this. I had super red hot and itchy rolling rashes. The rashes would show up in different places on my body and, within the hour, disappear. Our biggest organ is our skin, and when we are detoxing, many things come up to the surface so that they may finally leave. I was also having horrible migraines and would sleep for hours on hours. I think that my body needed that sleep with the great biological changes that it was undergoing because I had implemented many healing modalities. At first, I saw it as a bad thing, but then I also realized that sleep is extremely restorative. If you are going through a phase of extreme sleepiness as you explore these codes, that is all right. Give your body the rest it needs. I believe my headaches were my brain's way of telling me to rest. If you go through a healing crisis, whatever that may look like for you, marvel at the fact that it is happening. It can be hard to see at first that something that doesn't feel good is a good sign; however, it is. Your body is shifting its metabolic process to run more efficiently. It can just take time to readjust all your vast systems. Honoring your body through every change connects you more deeply to your body.

EMBODIMENT PRACTICE

1. Try out a form of detox this week. Connect with what your body feels and sit with any pain that may have been trapped in your body.

2. Start to note every product you use to become aware of what you are putting in your body and how you are creating your toxic load. Notice how in the list there are many "cleaning" products. It is important that you are not adding toxins to your body when you are in the act of cleaning. You want to be cleansing and cleaning at the same time. *Change any products listed to cleaner versions that feel right for you.*

Here is a small list that you can start with:

- *Toothpaste*
- *Shampoo*
- *Conditioner*
- *Body wash*
- *Lotion*
- *Laundry detergent*
- *Dish liquid*
- *Dish soap*
- *Makeup,*
- *Deodorant*

CHAPTER 3

Dance

Moving Your Body with Joy

NOW WE MOVE ON TO WHAT I CALL DANCE WHICH IS defined in this context as any way to get your body into movement. When we feel the most resistance to movement is when we need to move the most. You also don't have to do hardcore exercising to get the benefits of dance. I started by walking on a nature trail by my house. I used nature and subtle cardio to get my body moving. Eventually, I started dancing, yoga, and strength training. It is easier if you start small and then build up from there

It is extremely important that you have fun while moving your body. It is a way to get your blood pumping and get you into action. It is important that you, metaphorically and physically, just keep moving forward.

The name of this section is dance because it is a way to express yourself, have fun, and get yourself moving. You can use actual dancing in the dance section or any form of body movement that your body is craving. Dancing establishes movement and can be the start to connecting deeper to your body. I became so free when I started dancing like no one was in the room. (The fact that no one was there probably helped.) Dancing can be such an amazing practice for you to implement because you can help your entire body through dance. You can even make it fun and imagine that each of your cells are dancing with you. You can imagine them as little animated cartoons having a grand ole time. When we connect childlike imagination and childlike action into our routines, we allow ourselves to be free and deeply connected to our bodies. Dance to whatever music that you like because this method brings not only exercise and movement but also pure joy.

One form of exercise that is very common and highly effective is yoga. However, yoga is an interesting category because there is a wide variety of styles, methods, etc. The two main types of yoga I have learned are yin (feminine energy) and yang yoga (masculine energy). Yin yoga connects mind, body, and soul and utilizes breath during a few key poses. It is much more focused on stretch rather than strength. Yin yoga is how I started and is still my favorite because of the deep connection to my body. I suggest that anyone starting out do so with yin yoga because a lot of the westernized classes focus on yang yoga, and that is why many people say that yoga is not for them when in reality, they started off with the wrong type for them. At first, I was very resistant to yang yoga or vinyasa flows because I did not believe in my strength, and it wasn't what my body needed at the time. Once I became extremely connected to my body, I explored other forms of yoga.

When I started my health journey, I felt a lot of resistance to yoga because I heavily judged it and those who did it. I would get so angry when someone would suggest just to meditate or do yoga when I was in the depths of my pain because it felt like they were invalidating the pain I was in. I wanted to prove those people wrong by trying yoga and saying that it just wasn't for me. I wasn't doing practices that were good for me because I was desperate to have my pain validated. I had to choose yoga of my own volition. I had to choose a lifestyle that my soul was asking for and my body was craving.

I also learned that you could try yoga and really not try yoga. Yoga is an inward exploration. It connects you to the inner strength you didn't know existed. It is an inner ex-perience and not an outer representation. Yoga is mostly practiced using yoga poses (asanas). Still, yoga can be prac-ticed through any moment or non-movement that is done with purpose and is manifested from a conscious present decision. I invite you to allow yourself to explore move-ments that feel good for you, that align with what your body is asking for and what your soul is craving.

Cardio is another form of exercise that is crucial to this process, and that is because there are so many fun ways to do it. If you have fun every day, or most days, during your exercise routine, you are more likely to stay consistent with it, especially in the beginning phase. Your intention while doing exercise (or anything really) allows you to experience it differently. I highly suggest that you come to exercise with the mindset of, "I am doing this as an act of self-love, as a way to nourish me." Cardio doesn't have to be done in the gym but can be done while connecting to nature. This is another opportunity to create an environment for you not just to survive but thrive. The biggest myth with cardio is that you have to be sweating and do it until you are exhausted to get the benefits. Most people immediately think of running when they think of cardio. You can get an awesome cardio workout by playing tag, jumping on the trampoline, hula hooping, or some high-energy game. Other ways to do cardio include walking, hiking, swimming, etc. There are hundreds of different ways that you can perform cardio. You can explore this area and find what cardio you like. Whatever makes you feel that you are having a fun time is the best place to start.

Another consideration in the big categories of fitness is strength training. This may be an exploration for you because many different types of strength training range in intensity and form. There are multiple forms of "regular" strength training. Then there is high-intensity training, which uses all of your muscles for seconds to about a minute and then releases. This method is extremely efficient and effective. Strength training is a great addition, or it could be the main section of your workout routine. For me, I had to start walking to then graduate to yoga and resistance training. Whatever you find comfortable is good for you. Again, it is about the journey; you are consistently learning what types of exercise work for your body, which might change over time.

Now that you are aware that you do not have to go to the gym to get the benefits of exercise, let's discuss how the gym is a great resource for those that want to use it. If you plan on going to the gym, you want to have a game plan before going and sticking to it. Without a clear direction, you walk around aimlessly, wasting your precious time, your most valuable resource on this planet. Not only do you want to start with a game plan, but because you are building this as a lifestyle change and not a short-term habit, you need to start off slow and build yourself up.

You do not have to do an hour of exercise every day. You can do 15 minutes a day and start your day off right. We often do not exercise because we believe that working out means that we must be sweating, exhausted, and must have spent loads of time at the gym. Body movement and physical health, in general, are about consistent habits of small chunks of time so that you can integrate them into your life. Two hours at the gym is often not the best option for everyone. If that style works best for you, then go for it, but it is important to know that no single approach works for everyone. I trust you to follow your intuition about what works best for you and pick the approach that helps you integrate body movement into your life.

The "frequency" part of the dance section needs some special attention because it can be challenging to implement consistent habits (i.e., daily, weekly, monthly, etc.). To remedy this challenge, pick a time and stick to it. I suggest starting slow. Maybe start with one minute a day of some form of exercise and get it to 15 minutes in 15 days by adding one minute at a time. Then the next month, you might want to get it to 30 minutes a day or keep it at 15 minutes; it is all up to you.

Starting slow is crucial because of the acute phases or cycles one can get trapped in. These cycles can happen if you are a person who gets a gym membership and goes every day, for an hour daily for a week or two, and then gets tired. That phenomenon is completely normal because you just weren't being realistic when it comes to creating lifelong lasting habits. The trick is to start small, build on your habits, and be extremely intentional. True lifelong habits are easier to create when they are built on other habits. Getting some consistent exercise is way better than none. Starting really slow and building up is a great approach. Your holistically healthy habits will work with you and can grow with you as you grow as your exercise capacity increases.

In my life, I have given up because of acute overexertion. I have done this so many times. I wouldn't go to the gym at all, then a friend would invite me, and I would walk or run for four miles. I would be so sore the next day or a few days I wouldn't want to go again. Don't subconsciously sabotage yourself by going too hard when you first start going. If you need to start with just 15 minutes, that is amazing. That means you established the time you wanted to go, found time in your schedule, and just went. The more you do this, the more it becomes a habit. If you need to start with 15 minutes the first week and 20 minutes the second, you will be able to do a whole lot more benefit for your body. Optimizing your journey is all about building lasting habits, lifestyle changes, and intentional choices to proactively bring yourself into balance.

Sometimes you might start something and then realize that type of exercise is not for you. This does not mean that exercise, in general, is not for you. This is a misconception that your monkey mind might try to tell you—that if one form of exercise doesn't work for you, nothing will. As with any of these sections, your healthy habits adapt to you, your needs, and your current abilities. Do not become paralyzed in your life. Just start to move.

EMBODIMENT PRACTICE

Try out one form of exercise and commit to doing it at least one minute a day and scale up to the amount of time you believe will serve you. This form of scaling up movement allows for consistent celebration. We become more consistent in our dance practice when we are celebrated so make sure to celebrate yourself each step of the way.

Ex Try out Yin Yoga

Day 1:1 minute of Yin Yoga
Day 2: 2 Minutes of Yin Yoga
Day 3: 3 Minutes of Yin Yoga
Day 4: 4 Minutes of Yin Yoga
Day 5: 5 Minutes of Yin Yoga
Day 15: 15 minutes of Yin Yoga
Day 16: 15 minutes of Yin Yoga
Day 17: 15 minutes of yin yoga
Day 18: 15 minutes of Yin Yoga

BRINGING THE THREE D'S TOGETHER

YOUR RELATIONSHIP WITH YOUR BODY IS CRUCIAL TO living a vibrant life. Your body deserves your attention, affection, and commitment to it. It is fully devoted to you, which is why through your relationship with your body, you will naturally desire to have healthy habits. Not out of I have to or I should, but because you love your body and are deeply connected to it.

The three D's—Diet, Detox, and Dance—are an excellent way to express your devotion to your body. To have a healthy diet is to listen to your body and what it wants. It means looking through the lens of nourishing yourself and having a joyful intention while eating. A healthy diet is having an abundance of healthy food and knowing what your body doesn't want to consume. Detox is giving your body the breaks it needs to be able to get rid of stored toxins. It is cleansing the very vessel that allows you to live your life. You can also show your body love through dancing which is all about creating that connection to self through movement and making that expression of love to your body fun. It is having the intention of giving your body the environment it deserves to thrive in. These codes, infused with loving intention, connection to self, and joy, will radically change the way you associate embodying physical health. When you want to embody physical health because it feels so good and right, you will be exactly where you are supposed to be. When we think of health, we automatically think of the body. However, we have more to us. Our mental health is imperative to becoming healthy.

PART II
Embodying Vibrant Mental Health

THE POWER OF
YOUR MENTALITY

MY HEALING JOURNEY STARTED WITH MY INTENTION to heal my physical body. I was not aware at first that I would be doing it holistically, but I knew that I would use everything in my power to embody health. I followed my gut in whatever it said, and one day, my inner knowing had me searching for stamps. I felt this absolute need to find stamps, and I couldn't find them in a bin on the corner of our side table where they usually are. I said "forget it" at first, and I felt this urge that pulled me back to that corner. I didn't understand it, but I thought it had to do with the stamps I was trying to find. I started to get extremely frustrated. My mother was telling me to look in other places around the house, and I was pulled to that corner. Then I saw this little book that caught my eye, and relief washed over me. I didn't quite understand it, but I then read it, and it changed my life forever. This book is *The Four Agreements* by Don Miguel Ruiz[28].

This incredible book taught me not to say anything against myself, not to take things personally, not to make assumptions, and to always do my best. These concepts were revolutionary to me and, in practice, changed my life forever. I read the *Four Agreements* in one day, inhaling each word as it brought me back to life. This was when I started to heal physically and mentally, which cascaded into emotionally and then spiritually.

The Four Agreements also taught me a concept that I honestly had never consciously thought of before, which is the voice in my head. The author described it as a separate entity. Once I relearned this truth, it spoke to my soul. I felt immense relief. Because this voice is a separate entity, it is important to be unidentified from it. You are not your mind. Instead, it is a part of your human experience. Just because you have thoughts does not mean that you are your thoughts. Most spiritual texts say not to listen to the mind because of the addictions to loops and thoughts that do not serve you. The thoughts in your head come from your past. They use the lens of the past, and this is why they can be destructive to the present. The present moment is all there is in this life, and when this is mastered, life is mastered. I love this teaching of not listening to thoughts that run through my mind, and I practice it often. However, I like to create loving relationships with everything, which I did with my mind as well.

I also never thought that the voice in my head was so negative and against me. This realization taught me to become best friends with the voice in my head instead of it being my worst enemy. I started to read every book I could about this relationship I was trying to cultivate with myself. I didn't quite understand what it all meant. What did these books mean when they said that life is but a dream? What did they mean when they said we could choose what we wanted to believe? At first, I was confused, but as I noticed these things in my own life, I became enthralled.

It is important to make this voice in your head much kinder to yourself. How do you make that voice in your head your biggest cheerleader? A voice that is deeply in love and in awe of you. A voice that will encourage you and believe in your dreams. A space where you are free to dream the most extraordinary dreams for your life. These transformations are all possible, no matter where you are starting from. I went from the voice in my head being completely against me, paralyzing me, and reprimanding me repeatedly for my mistakes to hearing it speak with love, comfort, and forgiveness. I also can discern when to not listen to the voice in my head and when it is useful to use the mind as a tool to create an extraordinarily vibrant life. No matter what your relationship is with the voice in your head, know that it can improve drastically. It takes time, and you have to be kind to yourself on the way because isn't that the whole point? At first, I started to fall into this trap of "I am not being kinder to myself, and my thoughts are not kind to me" and then reprimanding myself for not being kind and for having unkind thoughts. Notice yourself throughout these exercises. If you are judging yourself for judging yourself, you will go down a rabbit hole that isn't much fun.

Now this isn't to say that you won't ever have an unkind thought in your head once you implement the three M's. However, it will be a drastically different experience. Awareness is key; observation is key. Once you become aware of the thoughts in your head, they can't hold power over you if you do not let them because you are looking at them through expanded consciousness.

Not only can our minds be flooded with thoughts, but they can also be flooded with mind movies. I would be wrapped up in the stories and movies that my mind would play. In Hebrew, there is a saying, "eating movies." You use this saying when your brain is taking you for mind loops. I deeply identify with this saying because for as long as I can remember, I was consuming the movies that would play in my head. It would get so intense that my body would make weird movements without my being aware of it at all. Extreme emotions would come to the surface. Or words would start to slip out of my mouth as I would entwine with the movie playing in my head. I feel most vulnerable to sharing this part of myself because I would be deeply embarrassed when someone would catch me awkwardly moving (I still am). I was so addicted to these mind movies that I would put my headphones in and walk around like a zombie, completely disconnected from the reality around me. It was an escape from reality and a prison of my own making. I would be deeply embarrassed when someone would ask me what I was doing, and I truly had no idea because my awareness was on the mind movies. This showed me that the mind-movies in my head had power over me.

Again, it would be remiss to say that I don't have daydreams or occasionally catch myself watching them intently and getting wrapped up in them, but I no longer choose to stay there, and I have way more awareness than before. I now use my power of daydreaming to fuel my power of visualization (which we will discuss in the Enrich chapter).

Holistic expression is when you become your own savior by making a collection of consistent habits that heal you, cleanse you, and get you ready to face any challenge or pain. It is not about never being unbalanced but how quickly you come back into balance and health. Mental health is not about never having a racing mind or having a mind movie play but having the tools to come back into the moment and master your mind.

EMBODIMENT PRACTICE

Start to become aware of your thoughts.

Are they kind to you, or are they unkind? Are they allowing you to live a full life? What are some repetitive thoughts you are having? Take note today on paper and write down the recurring thoughts you have during the day. Then survey whether or not you want to change the cycles that run through your head. You can use the question, "Does this thought serve me?" You must become aware of your thoughts to change them and have a healthy relationship with them.

CHAPTER 4

Mind Master

Mastering Your Inner Chatter

MIND MASTER IS WHEN YOU CAN CONSCIOUSLY choose your thoughts, which create your words, actions, and reality. To consciously choose these thoughts, you can reprogram your mind. This reprogramming changes your mind chatter, which is the voice or voices that are in your head. It comes down to the fact that your voices significantly influence your quality of life if you allow them to. If the voice in your head is constantly saying, "You will never feel better," you won't feel empowered enough to take action. There are many ways of going about this section because everyone is beautifully unique.

One way you can start to reprogram your mind is to interrupt thoughts and or beliefs that do not serve you. Why do I say reprogram? Our minds are like computers, and they follow a code, which is the computer's language. This code tells the computer what to do and what output to give if a certain stimulus is clicked. For example, you are going to have an immediate reaction to any given experience. If you have not consciously been picking your reactions, then your code has been written by others and will influence your immediate reactions. The "others" I speak of are your past experiences, society, those you surround yourself with, etc. By implementing Mind Master strategies, you will be able to reprogram your mind consciously, which will help you manifest your desires and dreams into reality.

Another way you can reprogram your mind is by interrupting disempowering thoughts. When a disempowering belief or thought comes up, you can say "I don't believe you" and replace it with an empowering thought or belief. You can tell the voice in your head, "I don't believe you," and fill up that space with something you want to believe. For example, if your mind says, "I am always going to be in pain," you can say aloud, "I do not believe you, and I choose to believe I am taking steps every day towards my abundance of health." You are here to reprogram your mind to continually empower you.

The voice or voices in your head can deliver many conflicting messages. Sometimes, they all seem to be screaming at you all at once. The one part I would like to focus on is the victim mentality. Victim mentality is seeing the world as if it is just happening to you and believing that everything that happens throughout the day is proof that your life sucks and you will always be in this pain. I am not saying that your pain isn't real because it very much is. However, I am giving you tools so that you don't have to feel like this anymore. You can choose to be empowered. You can choose to reprogram the voice in your head or simply not believe it when it says that you can't get the tangible results you desire. Your only real limitation in your life is the one you place on yourself through your conscious and subconscious thoughts.

Your mind voice can be against you, or it can be your biggest cheerleader. It all stems from your beliefs. What do you want to believe? Do you want to believe that it is more than possible to live any life you want? I am here to tell you, yes, you can, but you have to get that voice in your head on board or stop listening to what it says. You can also experience a journey of both, where you actively disbelieve the voice in your head until you have reprogrammed it to say thoughts that serve you.

For so long, I was allowing my pain to paralyze me. I did

this until I learned the harsh reality that "Pain is inevitable. Suffering is optional," as beautifully said by the Dalai Lama. Yes, I was in extreme pain, but to heal, I had to get out of that stuckness, that deep dark hole, no matter how hard it was. There are different ways to go about changing your mental chatter. Another form of reprogramming is through hypnosis, which can be used to change your beliefs. One of my good friends is a hypnotist, and he says that hypnosis is when you are in pure concentration. Hypnosis can also happen when a professional takes you to an altered state of consciousness and makes suggestions about anything you desire to reprogram. A hypnotist can help you believe that the glass of water you are drinking tastes like orange juice (crazy, right?). They can also support you in reprogramming your subconscious to believe that you are in charge of your life. Hypnotherapy is quite fascinating and can provide relief along with other modalities.

If you want to get an actual hypnotist, go for it, but there are also other options to try out. There are hypnosis videos or recordings which are usually most effective when you do a specific video every day for 30 days or more because it creates lasting change in your thought processes. You do not have to use the first track you find. You can search until one resonates with you and then use that one for 30 days. Ultimately, how long you listen to each track is up to you. Use your intuition to survey how long you should listen but do not mistake your intuition with resistance. If resistance is coming up for you when you are about to listen to the track, your mind is just afraid of any change. That means the track is producing a change, which in turn, is an indication that the track is beneficial to you.

Affirmations are also an excellent way to change those limiting beliefs and to become deeply empowered. MRI research in a 2016 study showed that affirmations strengthen neural pathways associated with positive self-evaluation and thoughts about oneself. This neural pathway change is a part of the goal of rewiring your brain to be kinder to yourself[29]. However, one important thing to remember about affirmations is that they only work if you truly believe them. You have to deeply believe that whatever you are declaring out loud is true. For example, I started off with, "I am getting better and better every single day." That is reasonable because It didn't have to be a huge leap but rather a small improvement. One day I looked back and said, "Woah, I have gone far." It is all about the baby steps.

There are many ways to practice using affirmations. The most popular statements are the "I am" statements. By cultivating an "I am" statement, you are allowing yourself to believe that you can become anything you set your mind to. "I am" statements are extremely powerful and provide deep resonating empowerment.

EXAMPLES OF I AM STATEMENTS

Physically	Mentally
I am free	I am peaceful
I am the embodiment of health	I am intentional
I am radiant	I am resilient
Emotionally	Spiritually
I am joyful	I am infinitely protected
I am loving	I am empowered
I am connected	I am guided

Another way to use affirmations is by using "I choose" or "I declare" statements. This is an empowering way to use affirmations because you are saying that you have a choice in the matter. It shows your subconscious mind the new belief that you are in charge of your reality and that you are choosing a new reality that serves your highest good. Making declarations to yourself is a powerful practice. When I took a new notebook and wrote down "Cassidy's Health Plan" I didn't know how I was going to do it but I knew that nothing was going to stop me. The power of a declaration can change the direction of your life in full alignment with your desire.

EXAMPLES OF CHOOSING STATEMENTS

Physically	Mentally
I choose health	I choose to have thoughts that are aligned to my vibrant self
I choose food that my body asks for	I choose to be intentional with what I consume
I choose to be in devotion to my body	I choose to be present

Emotionally	Spiritually
I choose self-love	I choose to have unshakable faith
I choose to forgive myself and others	I choose to surrender
I choose to live in gratitude	I choose to listen to my inner being

You can also make affirmations that are super-specific and are about your day. An example of these types of affirmations is, "I am going to replace old limiting beliefs with new empowering ones once a day." This is when you can get specific. These affirmations may be more believable based on where you are in your journey.

EXAMPLES OF SPECIFIC DIRECTION STATEMENTS

Physically	Mentally
I have the best health of my life because I eat at least one vegetable a day, exercise for 15 minutes a day and give my body the tools and resources to thrive	I manifest anything I desire into reality by reprogramming my thoughts and using affirmations weekly
I am deeply connected to my body because I take the time to listen to it	I am peaceful because I replace old limiting beliefs with new empowering ones once a day.
I am supported because I ask for help when I need it, especially when I am feeling overwhelmed, and my body is tensing from stress	I surround myself with people who empower me by being a part of powerful communities that are based on growth
Emotionally	Spiritually
I am authentically me with others; I have nothing to prove, hide or defend. I can say what I want, act how I want, and be who I want	I am guided because I take time to sit and intentionally listen to my intuition every morning

I am forgiving myself daily in the morning to clear up the energy of the day	I am present when I remind myself this moment is perfect
I am emotionally connected to myself because I check in with my emotions daily	I am protected and I look for evidence of this belief daily

If you need another low-risk place to start, use affirmations such as "I am willing to believe" or "I am learning how to." Maybe you have been in a disempowered state for a very long time, and when you say the other affirmations, you can't quite feel their power yet. This is when you start with "I am learning" affirmations.

EXAMPLES OF I AM LEARNING AFFIRMATIONS

Physically	Mentally
I willing to believe that movement can be joyful	I am willing to believe I can experience everything that I desire and I have everything I need to make that happen

I am learning how to celebrate myself during movement	I am learning to have thoughts that are aligned to my most vibrant self
I am learning how to listen to my body	I am learning to be kinder to myself
Emotionally	**Spiritually**
I am willing to believe that my pain can be transformed into peace	I am willing to believe that I am protected and loved unconditionally
I am learning how to embrace each emotion with love	I am learning to connect to my higher power
I am learning how to live in gratitude	I am learning to surrender

To go further into cellular belief, if you feel you do not believe the statements above, then a deeper form of affirmations is imperative. By asking questions, you allow yourself to be open to more belief because you are starting from a place of disbelief. This type of affirmation is where you ask questions to yourself. Instead of asking yourself, "Why is this happening to me?" you can ask yourself, "What would it take to create a vibrant life?" Or you can go even a step further and ask, "How can I become the embodiment of health?" When you ask, "How can I?" it becomes a matter of when, not if. Your brain is consistently looking for evidence, and if you ask out loud *why*, *how*, and *what would it take* questions, your brain will look for the answers because it is constantly looking for evidence.

EXAMPLES OF AFFIRMATION QUESTIONS

Physically	Mentally
What would it take to find healthy habits that bring me into balance?	Why am I so lucky in my life?
How can I increase my vitality?	How can I be more present?
How can I give my body the tools and environments for it to thrive?	What is possible for me to create this month?

Emotionally	Spiritually
What would it take to truly feel empowered?	Why am I on the right path?
I am learning how to embrace each emotion with love	I am learning to connect to my higher power
What would it take to live vibrantly?	What would It take to trust myself, my life, and my higher power?

Your brain is extremely powerful. You can be in charge of it, or it can be in charge of you. This is when you have to decide which will be true for you. How will you stay the most consistent when it comes to affirmations? Follow your intuition, not the voice in your head that says you don't need to do it. Try it and see how you feel. A deep part of you needs to hear what you are saying out loud. Make sure to state these affirmations out loud and proud and believe your empowering words.

Once you use these reprogramming tools, you can believe in what serves you. You can take any criticism with a grain of salt. Imagine utilizing the amazing power of the brain to intentionally visualize the future you want to bring into form. It is an incredible feeling, but there is no destination to this. There is not one day where you say, "Ah yes, I am mentally healed now, I can stop doing all the work that I am doing," because what you are doing is proactively personifying health. I am presenting each item in this book as a complete lifestyle change. These are all muscles that you will need to work out to keep strong. It is like exercise for the brain. You don't just go to the gym once and expect results. You keep going to get those desired muscles and have to keep going to maintain them. Affirmations, however, are usually a very short practice and can be done daily. If you only want to do them once a week or twice a week, that is up to you to decide. It is all up to you and what you can hold yourself accountable to. This practice does get easier with time; however, starting your journey with affirmations can be powerful because they allow you to take inspired action. Once you start seeing wonderful results from these exercises, it is much easier to maintain a higher level of mental health. It is harder to start, but it will become more effortless to practice once you find your rhythm.

EMBODIMENT
PRACTICE

1. Your intuition is a beautiful thing. If you ask it empowering questions, you will receive empowering answers and results. Ask yourself empowering questions and watch the magic unfold from there.

2. Journal on the difference between your inner knowing and your programmed thought patterns. What thought patterns do you want to develop? Pick or create an affirmation that goes along with this goal and speak it every day for 30 days.

CHAPTER 5

Mind Diet

Intentional Mind Consumption

WHEN YOU THINK ABOUT DIETS, YOU USUALLY THINK about food, but there is so much more to it. Rather, it is everything that you consume, including the information you absorb, relationships you experience, and environments you are immersed in. Your health is affected by these aspects immensely in ways that you may not have noticed before. You may have never consciously thought about your mind diet, but it has real implications on your overall health.

ENVIRONMENT

The first part of your mental diet is the environment you choose to be in. What is a room that you spend most of your time in? Is it clean and tidy or a disaster zone? What does your house say about your mind? Do you feel that you are just tolerating what your environment feels like? Have you wanted to decorate for so long but never gotten around to it? Is your environment at work conducive and encouraging for you to be creative? Do you put yourself in environments that reset you instead of drain you? These questions are meant to get you conscious about the environments you place yourself in. This is a judgment-free zone so that you can stand in your naked truth.

The first way you can create mental health through your mind diet is to declutter and decorate your spaces to bring you peace and joy and cultivate creativity. Think of all of the spaces you use daily, i.e., your bedroom, office, car, etc. These are all places that you can make into your own.

During my awakening journey, I decided to declutter everything I no longer needed. I was astonished at the sheer amount of clutter that I had. I gave away over eight trash bags filled with clothes that no longer fit and those I had not worn in years. I gave away three bags of books that I read and no longer read the genre. I had so many trinkets and things that I felt attached to, and I decided at that moment that my room being decluttered was more important than these weird attachments to things that added no value to my life. I got rid of seven trash bags filled with trinkets and random items. I had no idea how truly cluttered my room was until I decluttered it. It felt liberating to get rid of so many items. I asked myself if I had used something in the last year, and if I hadn't, I threw it out. If I am not using an item within a year, it is a strong indicator that I'm not going to use it. The other vital question I asked was, "Does this bring value to me?" If I said no, I also gave it away. There were even a few items that I found that I brought into use because I forgot they were there, and now they bring value to me. I then painted my bedroom a very light periwinkle, and I put up pretty lights and decorated it so that it felt like a place of serenity. I wanted my outside environment to reflect what I wanted to feel on the inside.

When I wake up in the morning, I get to feel the serenity that I created for myself. I make sure that my space is clean because it is my haven. I make sure everything is decluttered and start my day right. I was the absolute messiest person you have ever met, and if you feel like, "Oh well, I am just a messy person," I challenge you to examine that statement. I said it too, and then I adopted a new identity of a person that does whatever is necessary to feel peaceful and blissful. Creating a conducive environment for peace was vital to my activation journey. Decluttering and a new coat of paint can make a world of difference. I noticed the effects immediately. I started waking up and seeing what I did for myself, and I was just so proud and in awe that I had changed my environment. I never in my life had painted rooms before, and I even found that task to be relaxing. It took one week to declutter, one week to paint, and one week to decorate. Like I said, these changes did not happen overnight, but I took more and more action geared toward expressing my love for myself. I look back now and see that all the baby steps I took made a huge difference collectively.

What rooms in your life do you want to change? Do you want to change your office? Do you want to change any rooms of yours to feel serene? What place in your house feels so cluttered that you know once that is cleaned up, you will feel lighter and relieved? What items are you allowing in your life that no longer bring your value?

By changing your environment, you are being extremely intentional about what you want to feel in your life and creating a new environment that can foster that growth and change. This process will be a little uncomfortable because it has a lot to do with change. But, it will be so worth it when you start to realize how amazing you feel and the transformation your life has taken because you were able to do something that is seemingly so little. I am going to remind you, again and again, that this is your journey: fashion it to fit your life and allow you the most transformation. This is the time in your life to commit to yourself because you deserve to put yourself first. If you haven't put yourself first in a long time, it is even more imperative to make your life about you. Being selfish is actually being selfless because it allows you more unconditional love to offer the world. What are you going to get rid of to invite the energy of peace? How are you going to create environment(s) for yourself? What type of environment(s) are you going to choose to be in?

RELATIONSHIPS

Choosing your environments can also be who you surround yourself with and what these relationships look like. Are your relationships built on love or fear? Do you feel filled up or drained after interacting with someone close to you? Are healthy boundaries set in your relationships? Do you give from your overflow, or do you give until you have nothing left? These powerful questions will help you start thinking about how you are co-creating the dynamics in your relationships, which have real implications for your health and well-being.

To make you feel even more comfortable, I will show you the answers I started to write as I self-reflected, so you don't feel alone if you start realizing you have answers you don't like. The first question allowed me to sit down and see which relationships were built on love or fear. The ones built on fear are the ones I was terrified of losing because of deep attachments, codependency, fear of being lonely, and fear of being abandoned. The ones built on love allowed me to feel free., I didn't have to worry about trusting them. I would feel filled up and truly loved by the person. The third question got me to see that I did not hold healthy boundaries with others and, in turn, was teaching them to take more than I could give and to expect my energy to be easily accessible to them. Once I started to notice that I had absolutely no boundaries, it felt like a big slap in the face. I also gave until I had nothing left to give, and I would go through immense breakdowns that caused much turmoil in my life.

Once I started to ask myself these questions, I became more self-aware of how I was relating to others. Through immense reflection, I realized that I was teaching others how to treat me. Someone can only treat you the way that you allow them to. This was a big blow to my ego at first because I allowed myself to be a continuous victim. It is as if I was addicted to being the one that was right and also treated poorly. I was attached to these ideas and cycles without even realizing it. I would continue to attach myself to people with whom I no longer had healthy dynamics because of these unconscious addictions.

Your relationship with others is crucial in how you relate to the world. Humans are social creatures, and finding deep bonds with others helps with the feelings of safety. Often when a relationship of attachment is burst, we experience a sense of unsafety. It is hard to feel safe or trust in life and yourself in these moments. When you don't trust others, it is because you do not trust yourself not to make the same mistakes that made you in past relationships in the first place. This is the first clue that you co-create your relationship dynamics and or cycles that you may feel trapped in. I am here to tell you that you have more power in your relationships than you may believe. You have the power to who has access to you and what that access looks like. You have the power to create the relationships that fill you up and that are healthy.

In an awakening journey, you inevitably become much more conscious and intentional about what you allow in your life. If you meet your own needs, you can create deep bonds with others instead of deep attachments. You can then love people exactly as they are and let go if they are no longer meant to be in your life. During this journey, you may become unattractive to the people stuck in unconscious patterns, but you will attract others who are living their lives consciously. You will then attract the relationships that allow you to love from your overflow and not relationships that drain you. The decision to love from your overflow, however, is a decision you must make over and over again.

This transition of putting your needs first so that you may love in your overflow takes lots of practice. If you have the habit of giving, giving, and giving, and leaving nothing for yourself, this may take time. Let me put into perspective why loving yourself first is so imperative. If you love from your overflow, you do not look for others to fill your needs and desires. In the past, you may have become resentful when you give energy to someone, and they do not give the energy you believe you deserve back. Your relationships may become a toxic cycle of you giving your all and them not reciprocating, leaving you angry and sad. You start to resent the person you love because you have given everything to them. Does this sound familiar? If it does, then it is time to put yourself first so that you give from your overflow and anything anyone else gives you is extra blessings. Through this practice, wonderful healthy dynamics for your relationships allow you to be more fulfilled by them. As you become more aware of these habits that no longer serve you, you can break the toxic cycles you may be in.

Your relationships with others need to be a healthy exchange between both people. Are there any relationships that are just absolutely draining you? Then it might be time to detox your friendships or any other relationships in your life that aren't good for your health. Or you can detox unhealthy toxic patterns. You can do this by recreating those dynamics with someone you have in mind by setting healthy boundaries. You might create some turbulence by creating these boundaries because perhaps others have relied on your generosity. The person you may have in mind might disagree with the new dynamics. This is when you then find a way to focus only on yourself and possibly find a way to end this relationship, as the other person may be attached to toxic patterns that you are trying to release. Your job is to take care of your body, mind, and soul. Sometimes other people can act as poison to us because they are poisoning themselves with their sadness and unconscious patterns. This does not mean that you need to go out and cut off all the people in your life if you are in a fight or a little bit of a rut. I am talking about those relationships you have genuinely given your all to and that are not healthy for either of you. These relationships are stuck in a cycle where you feel your boundaries have been crossed repeatedly. Instead of cutting people out, try first to set clear, healthy boundaries and experiment to see how that plays out. Relationship detoxes are key to your health because when you are releasing all of the old toxic habits of your past, you realize that you do not want to repeat them. When you become more conscious of your life, you notice that you were blind to your own power in your relationships. By releasing relationships or cycles, you can fully embody health at a whole other level.

You have to change how you co-create experiences with others because if you cut people off and do not change how you show up in a relationship, you will create that same relationship again, just with a different person. You teach people how to treat you. If someone new comes into your life and you teach them to treat you the same as before that is the same relationship with a new person and you are stuck in a cycle. This is why so many people find themselves attracting the same partner or the same friendship. This, in turn, perpetuates "proof" of their belief that they can't trust people and that everybody is the same. These people don't realize that it is only through the self that change will happen.

When I first heard that I was giving my power away, I was so angry. I would say, "That is not true, and this person does not know my situation." Well, I am here to lovingly tell you the truth, that you need to take your power back because you have given it to far too many people. You need that power to wield self-love. Your body, mind, and soul will be so much cleaner with healthy relationships in your life.

Your friends may or may not want you to continue some unhealthy habits and actions because they do not want to feel alone in doing them. If your friends try to convince you and don't quite understand, it is ok; it is not up to them to understand what you are doing right now. It is for you to put your needs for your health above your need to be accepted. More often than not, if you have good friendships, your friends will drop it and say "ok" when you are firm with your choice. You take immense pressure off yourself when you shift from doing what others want you to do to being authentically you. Being true to yourself is one of the healthiest things you can do because it means that you are not drinking the poison of social pressure.

There are so many toxins and poisons that you have consumed and stored on a deep level. When people think of trauma, they often imagine these traumas to be huge and catastrophic. However, traumas can be covert and under-the-radar yet deeply affect your life. Often, the little things can make a significant impact because they can accumulate over time. This is why little incidents in any relationship can make a big difference in your health and life.

Your relationship with others should fill you up with love, not poison. Relationships in your life should not drain you so much that you have no love to give yourself. It is time to cleanse your life and create an environment in which vitality is inevitable. You should be able to identify who in your life fills you up with love and whom you feel extremely supported by. Those are the people you should be hanging out with more. If you do not feel you have these people, then it is imperative that you attract the people that support you by choosing to support yourself.

In your relationships, remember these four actions: be conscious about what interactions you allow in your life, give yourself what you need so that you love in your overflow, create healthy boundaries, and be conscious about patterns that do not serve you so that you may release them. Loving from your overflow and keeping relationships in your life that add value will exponentially change your life. You want your relationships to help you on your journey. The people in your life should be your cheerleaders, creating a support system to aid your healthiest reality.

This detox of your relationship patterns may look like recreating relationship dynamics, hanging out with some people more, less or not at all. This process may look like making new friendships where you start to teach them the real way you want to be treated. All in all, it begins with you.

INFORMATION

An information diet is all about everything you consume, including books, tv shows, and social media. In this generation, there is consistent information overload. There is so much information out there that can be extremely valuable and, on the other hand, so much that can poison you. What you consume is up to you. You may have never thought about your information diet before because thinking for yourself and choosing the reality we desire to live in is not taught in schools. You may have never consciously asked yourself if the meme you are consuming is adding value to your life. You can allow others to choose what you consume or not, or you can intentionally consume what you believe will add value to your life.

One information stream that I want to bring special attention to is social media. This one can be a useful tool or take over your life. Ask yourself: Is this bringing me value? What is my intended outcome from consuming this piece of content? When I asked myself this, I got so frustrated because I had to be honest with myself. I was using social media unintentionally and was on social media for hours at a time. I didn't have a great relationship with social media. I was so attached that I would do social media cleanses where I would delete my apps for a few weeks and then become completely addicted again. I did these detoxes for a couple of years, but I always seemed to fall back into the same bad habits—scrolling for hours, getting upset when a person from the past posted something, complaining about something in my life, etc. It was a cycle that I was stuck in. While I was learning to embody mental vibrancy, I asked myself what my intention was when using social media and what value I got from it. My intention and value came from connecting to others and inspiration. That is when I started to realize I needed to change my feed. Notice how our social media companies even use the word feed. Your feed on social media is what you are consuming for your mind to digest, and it is imperative that you consciously choose what you are feeding your mind.

My intentions produced huge results. My screen time used to average around 16 hours a day, and after I made changes to my social media, it decreased to three hours a day. I had completely changed my social media feed. I unfollowed every account that posted something that I did not resonate with or was not going to help me live the life I desired. Did it have me delete a few funny video accounts? Yes, it did. It was way more worth it than I ever realized. I also created a time limit of 30 minutes a day. That is the amount of time that I deemed the most valuable time frame. I can connect with people through DM's, I can share valuable content, and I can scroll just a little bit to get intentional value. I don't check my social media until around noon. I also don't use my phone for two to three hours after waking up and one to two hours before bedtime. At first, I thought that doing this would be so extreme.

For ten years, I would wake up and immediately touch my phone. I used to be super cranky in the morning, but now I wake up feeling refreshed. I allow myself to have built-in me time, which has been crucial to embodying health at all levels and dimensions. When I wake up now, I get to create thoughts that are in my highest good instead of consuming information that can start my day off on the wrong foot. I also discovered that I am highly creative when I first wake up. It is a time for me to make artistic expressions (such as writing this book). This transition took a while to get used to, but I am so thankful to myself for creating these new habits. You, too, will thank yourself for having this built-in self-only time in the mornings or evenings.

First, I invite you to set a limit for yourself. How long do you want to be spending on your social media? There is no judgment here, however long you want to pick. I am asking you to be conscious about how much screen time you use. You may be surprised about the sheer amount of time you spend on these apps. It is also not your fault that you may be scrolling for hours, as social media is created to be addictive. Creating time limits allows you to become more conscious about how you are using your time, giving you the opportunity to make a different choice. Another way you can completely change how you use social media is by changing your feed. You want to unfollow all of the accounts that no longer serve you and give you a bad feeling. You then replace them with the information you consciously choose to consume. You want people and messages that inspire you and get you off your phone and into action. These steps, without a doubt, have the potential to change your life.

Changing the people and pages you follow on social media can be a healing experience. You might feel a tinge of hurt when you see people from your past appear in your feed. Sometimes you just don't know why you are following people who have nothing to do with your life. Getting rid of some of these people made me realize that I have control over my feed and life. This single action can completely change your life for the better. I know it might seem scary to "delete people," but you are putting yourself first, which is the most important part. This is your time to put yourself first and only allow the people and things that fill you up instead of drain you.

Now ask yourself the questions that have the power to change your life forever. When answering these questions, think about social media and all other channels through which you consume information.

What value am I getting out of this? How can this app bring me value? What is my intention when I spend my time, my most valuable resource, here? What is my intention when I post this? What is my intention when I spend more than 15 minutes at a time? Is this something I choose to consume consciously? If I consume this information, will it serve me and the life I desire to live? Is this healthy consumption?

I am not telling you to do anything that I do not do myself and consistently. I do not preach unless I practice. Is it difficult? Yes, but it has the potential to bring positive change into your life.

EMBODIMENT
PRACTICE

Journal on these two questions.

1. What have you been consuming in the areas of relationship, environment, and information that you think is detrimental to your health?

2. What can you consume more regularly that resonates with your most vibrant health?

CHAPTER 6

Mindfulness

Being Present

MINDFULNESS IS THE ACT OF BEING COMPLETELY PRESent in the moment, and it is the most crucial piece to this vibrancy jigsaw puzzle. I know I say that about almost every section here, but truly living in the moment will change your life forever. Putting mindfulness into practice is not an easy feat, but it is so well worth it. Let me also note that you cannot be mindful all the time. Your mind will take you away from the present moment, but the point of mindfulness is more about recognizing when your mind is taking you away and choosing to come back to the present.

Mindfulness is key because it is a new way of living. It is a way to live in the here and now. Learning mindfulness at first might feel weird, but you'll feel liberated when you are fully immersed in the present. Mindfulness is the way to get out of the cycle of constantly worrying about the past and future and just be.

You can start to practice mindfulness by telling yourself this moment is perfect. If you have any tension in your body, you will feel it melt away while saying this beautiful statement. This mantra is a great tool to actively relax and reduce your stress. By reminding yourself and your body that you are safe, you activate the parasympathetic nervous system, which is the opposite of your stress response, also known as your sympathetic nervous system.

The most known way to practice mindfulness is by meditation. Now you may already practice frequently, rarely, or not at all. Wherever you are right now is a great starting place. I hear the phrase "I am just not good at meditation" all the time. I laugh at this sentiment because meditation is not a test; there is no way to do better or worse. It is simply being. The point of meditation is also skewed in your brain so that you resist doing it. Meditation is not about completely clearing your mind; it is about being in the moment and being intentional about what you feel, think, and act on. To focus on the moment, you divert your energy and attention from your thoughts, but that does not mean that your intruding thoughts will completely disappear. Like a computer, they may be running in the background, but you can notice them and let them go. When most people get frustrated with meditation, it is because they want to do it perfectly when there is no such thing.

For example, when I first tried meditation, years before my accelerated awakening journey, it used to be either boring or hard. I would feel relaxed after, but sometimes it felt like grueling work to calm my mind because it was always so active, and my natural state was anxiety. Relaxing was hard for me through mindfulness practices; however, I tried something new. I became consistent. I put myself in a course with daily, live, 15-minute meditations. Because these meditations were live, I felt accountable to attend every morning, Monday through Friday. Through consistent meditation practice, I started to see the real benefits. Consistency in mindfulness transformed my natural state into one of bliss and joy; anxiety became an unfamiliar experience. I noticed immense benefits from my meditation practice, such as positive thought patterns and the elimination of brain fog and forgetfulness.

To me, meditation feels like an internal massage or an internal cleansing as I deeply intertwine with the present moment. It now feels that my body is cooling down, a feeling that radiates from my heart to melt and relax the rest of my body. My whole body softens and vibrates; it is the most amazing feeling. I know this experience takes a while to get to, but through consistent practice, it is a possibility that is within you right now. Sometimes during my practice, I become deeply connected to the parts of me that I was resisting, which brings up repressed emotions. Many people unconsciously avoid meditation because of fear of feeling pain. However, all of these emotions need to be processed in the present moment to be released. If you are struggling to meditate, keep at it. Over time you can have new experiences with it. As with everything, it is about taking a baby step at a time and being consistent.

Meditation and mindfulness have been hot areas of study in the past decade. These spaces are growing faster and faster, showing more benefits every day. Some of these studies include helping with emotional stability[30], increasing compassion for self and others[31], reducing blood pressure[32], reducing pain[33], reduced inflammation[34], increased self-awareness[35], etc. After reading many neuroscience studies on the immense benefits of meditation, some of which completely blew my mind, I knew that it was going to be a key ingredient in my recipe for health. Research shows that after only eight weeks of constant meditation, your brain changes its shape and function! Those who go through an eight-week meditation and mindfulness program had MRIs done on them and found that the brain density decreased in the amygdala, which is the center that deals with fear, anxiety, and stress. Another part of the brain, the hippocampus, showed to be larger. This area of the brain deals with memory and emotional processing[36]. One particular neural pathway that is reduced with a meditation practice is called the default mode network, which is where your thoughts take you away unconsciously and where daydreaming occurs[37]. Research has also shown that regular meditators have a different natural brain wave state, which is associated with greater levels of happiness[38]. Mental, emotional, physical, and spiritual well-being can be drastically improved with this one consistent practice. Meditation is the foundation and space where many codes can unlock vibrancy.

There are so many different ways to explore meditation and mindfulness. There is no one right way to meditate. Lots of companies will say theirs is the best and I have heard the advice to stick to one method and only do it that way. I disagree. Through my observations, I have noticed that those who switch up their meditation routine variably have more fun in their journey because they are practicing childlike exploration. Try out a bunch of different mindfulness and meditation practices because one technique might bring more benefits to you one day and a different one the next. Once you can enter altered brain wave states on your own, you can see immense benefits from meditation without the assistance of guided meditation. Meditation then can become how you live your life, ever present.

Another way to practice mindfulness is to practice intention for each thought you have, each word you speak, and each action you take. Having an intention is choosing the exact outcome you want by practicing your creative power. Being intentional allows you to cultivate the life you deeply desire. Mindfulness will enable you to create a life in the here and now. These intentional choices in every area of your life create freedom because you practice your autonomy or your ability to create your reality.

There are many times in my life when I was doing something that was the opposite of what I wanted. For example, something came out of my mouth that was opposite to what I meant. Or I did something out of anger that created the opposite result of what I wanted to happen. I would push someone away when I really wanted them to be close and for us to connect. It did not make sense.

This behavior was a result of my unconscious patterns, but by being mindful of my choices, I was able to break those cycles. You can break any cycle you may feel stuck in using this mindful choice-making.

For example, saying "I am fine" and expecting someone else to figure out that you are mad is not the way to get what you want. If you want to make up with someone and act as if you never want to see this person again, then your actions and intentions are not aligned. Now again, there is a balance because there is no black and white. Anger is a valid feeling, but we can act with integrity and intention in these moments. Also, you may often be angry about someone crossing a boundary, but you did not set it clearly. If you feel a boundary has been crossed, first make that boundary clear to the other person. Do your best to say what you mean and align your actions with your intention. Becoming conscious of your intentions can help change these cycles you may be stuck in, affecting many areas of your life. If you want to change a particular outcome in your life, then change the habits around that area. As Einstein said, "Insanity is when you do the same thing over and over again and expect different results." Now, it is time to make changes that create lasting results.

You can also practice mindfulness when you observe

your environment and ask questions about what you see, hear, and feel. You can bring back your childlike curiosity and exploration. It may be hard for you at first to tap into that younger version of you that was so immersed in the moment and that had a deep desire to make an adventure out of almost anything. Do you remember that part of you, and can you express it in the here and now? You can also just observe and notice your environment's different colors, patterns, textures, and sounds.

In almost every healing modality you explore, you practice mindfulness or being fully present in the moment. Some of these codes combine and synergize to give you the highest benefit for your multidimensional health. A great deal of these different health modalities are placing you in the moment, so technically, they can all be considered a way to practice mindfulness and be fully present in the moment. Also, meditative practices are so wide-ranging and different that sometimes you don't even know when you are practicing. Forewarning, don't use this synergy as a cop-out to not meditate because it can be difficult sometimes to sit down and intentionally meditate. Allow yourself to explore this area and give yourself permission to "not do it right" so you may find all of the benefits.

EMBODIMENT PRACTICE

Try out one meditation type.

Having this time with yourself cultivates a
mind-body-spirit connection where you can
hear the messages from your inner intelligence
much louder. I always suggest trying it out for
five to fifteen minutes daily for at least eight to
12 weeks. This is when you can see the immense
benefits of meditation.

BRINGING THE THREE M'S TOGETHER

The benefits are abundant when you use the three Ms; Mind Master, Mind Diet, and Mindfulness. Mind Master is when you reprogram your thoughts to be loving so that they serve the reality you desire to live. It is becoming best friends with the voice in your head and holding healthy boundaries with it. When you embody the Mind Diet code, you are extremely intentional about what you allow yourself to consume, whether information consumption, environment consumption, or relationship consumption. What you consume will consume you, and wouldn't you rather that be love, peace, and serenity? Mind Diet helps you become conscious about thinking through what you consume to further master your mind.

Through Mindfulness, your life will forever change by being present in every moment. Mindfulness is about fully living life and continuing to master the mind because it allows you to discern when to use the mind and when being present serves you more. Being present is the modality that has the most power in your life if you allow it. Embodying vibrant mental health is a never-ending process, which may seem daunting, but these lifestyle changes can transform your life for the better. It can be so hard to start all of these habits, but once you do, the magic starts to happen in your life, making you want to continue these beautiful habits. You become freer and freer as you exercise your mental muscles; it is almost like you are learning to fly or lift the weight of the past and future off your shoulders. Either way, you are much lighter.

A warning that I am going to provide here is that when you start to sit with yourself in meditation or mindfulness, old feelings and wounds may emerge. You may have never sat with yourself before without avoiding your feelings. Do not feel bad if you do this because this is extremely common. Most people in our society are constantly "doing" things so that they may avoid feelings that come up. However, this hinders connection to self, your ability to embody mental health, and your ability to receive. If you are closed off from yourself, you are closed off from the world. When you sit with yourself, you no longer can run away from the connection to your emotions that needs to occur. In the next section, we will discuss dealing with these emotions when they arise during some of your embodying mental health practices.

PART III
Embodying Vibrant
Emotional Health

THE POWER
OF YOUR
EMOTIONALITY

THE TIME I SPENT BECOMING MENTALLY HEALTHY showed me just how emotionally dysfunctional I was. When I sat and observed myself, I saw that I would actively avoid many of the feelings that came up. I had not dealt with so much of my life emotionally. I would stuff everything into a bottle until I became a volcano and erupted with anger and tears. I would avoid my feelings at such a deep level that I stuffed them away until my nervous system got fried. I would have anxiety, panic attacks, and emotional outbursts. Because I was not emotionally healthy, I would have these panic attacks that would wake me out of my sleep just to be in a panic. I had no real emotional stability even though I made it seem that I did. I constantly tried to control my feelings and avoid the bad ones, creating a dysfunctional relationship. Are you starting to notice a trend? We have relationships with just about everything in our life, including our emotions, and it is up to us how we co-create these dynamics.

I was in terrible cycles where my resentment for others would burst out and when my self-abandonment would become too much to handle. I never used these opportunities of bursting (mini-crises) to my advantage to deal with my past traumas, but I did use my holistic exploration to do that for me, which started from a major crisis. Those feelings that I kept stuffing away still lived in my body, mind, and spirit. I just continued to bury them under clouds so that I would be unconscious of them. Emotional healing is about digging out those past emotions and processing them in a safe place so that you may let them go.

The seasons where we make the greatest lasting changes are the ones when we are in pain. Your suffering is an opportunity to let deep, lasting healing begin; however, you do not need to be suffering to decide to connect deeper to yourself and your life and create a quality of life beyond your wildest imagination. Your future is in your hands. This is where you take charge and say, "No more will I ignore parts of myself that are meant to be loved, felt, and cherished; no more will I take the actions that do not serve my health and my highest good." This is the time you choose to live your life and or choose to use your pain to create an even happier and healthier version than you have ever been. Are you ready to confront these emotions that may feel uncomfortable? I remember at first, I was scared. I asked myself, "What if I go into a deep dark hole of depression by feeling my feelings? What if it doesn't help?" We often avoid pain at all costs. It takes a lot of conscious choices to change the dynamics of your emotions and emotional regulations. Many do not believe that they can heal themselves because they do not believe in their innate abilities or their capacity to create a safe place for this unfolding.

Doubt is where many people falter because it stops them from trying. This skepticism usually comes from the belief that one pill, one treatment, or one diet will end all of their suffering. It can be devastating when a single cure doesn't work or doesn't work fully. Embodying health is a journey; it is not a destination. Journeys are filled with exploration. Letting go of the attachment to the outcome and immersing yourself in the journey will be very beneficial, if not crucial.

We also experience resistance because, in our society, there is this falsehood of being strong which is not showing your "weak emotions." When we suppress our emotions, they come bursting out in ways that do not serve us. There is also a disconnect when we label emotions as good or bad. Each emotion is there for you and is not against you. An act such as crying can be therapeutic because it is a form of release. Our society suffers a long history of deeming some emotions lesser than or not real. Emotions are sometimes associated with women and their suppression. Women were—and still are—characterized by the terms "crazy," "emotional," and even "hysterical." Being emotional is then connected to suppression and invalidating the experience of feeling. That is why many feel that they are crazy or not being of the right mind when they have many heavy emotions. Men especially suffer in this area because they are not allowed to feel these "feminine" emotions. It becomes harmful to have this subconscious programming; however, it can be remedied by consciously creating a healthy relationship with your emotions, which can be accomplished using the three E's: embrace, enrich, and evolve.

Having an emotional connection to self allows you to have emotional mastery. You realize that you are in charge of your emotions when you deeply allow them to be felt. I am so happy to say that I am no longer in a constant state of anxiety, and I have not had one panic attack since learning to connect to my emotions. Once you realize the responsibility for your own emotions, you no longer look to others to make you feel happy, fulfilled, or content, which allows you to have deep emotional connections to others. Your vulnerability and authenticity with yourself unlock a new level of emotional intelligence that enhances your ability to connect. Once you unlock levels of emotional intimacy with yourself, you unlock new levels that allow you to emotionally connect with another person or the people in your life. Having an emotional connection to yourself affects you and everyone around you.

Emotional healing allows you to clear up the past, connect to yourself and others on a deeper level, and create your future. We manifest our life through the art of feeling. When you have a vision for yourself, manifestation comes from your feelings. You find more drive in your life when you let your emotions be a motivator. Emotions are what allow you to create a vision that you truly desire. Desire is a beautiful emotion that holds power in your life for great manifestation. It is not the same as wanting because wanting comes from attachment to some outside reality, while desire is the burning flame that your soul wants to experience. When you become connected to your emotions, you can then survey whether that vision is something you want, which comes from the feeling of scarcity, or if it's something you desire deep in your soul, which comes from the feeling of abundance. The deeper the connection to your emotions, the more you allow them to co-create a beautiful reality with you.

When you connect with your emotions, you may also understand and discern the feelings that you need to feel and the messages that come from your inner knowing. Creating a relationship with yourself goes so much deeper when you start to have a healthy relationship with all parts of yourself. In this human experience, all feelings are meant to be felt. When you love your emotions and connect with them, you get to feel the relief of having some mastery of them. You are not trying to control them but instead are working with them.

EMBODIMENT PRACTICE

Journal on these questions:

1. Ask yourself whether you are avoiding any feeling(s).

2. If so, which ones? Why are you avoiding them?

3. What gifts or lessons have you received in the past from these feelings?

4. Are you ready to embrace all expressions of the human experience?

CHAPTER 7

Embrace

Holding Space for All Your Feelings

EMBRACING YOUR EMOTIONS IS WHEN YOU RECEIVE
them openly and lovingly so you may let go or transmute
them. The embrace category sounds easy, but it is one of
the hardest codes to embody. Your brain wants to protect
you from feeling pain, but it also distracts you when you
feel a heavy emotion.

Embracing each emotion or event in your life is crucial to letting them go and transmuting them. Otherwise,
they will bubble up and become even stronger because you
tried to push them down. I have been there, and you have
probably been there too. Our society teaches us that being
strong is silencing our emotions. However, having a good
cry might be the strongest action you can take.

If you choose to run away from any feeling, you won't be able to get the message that you need from your body. Each emotion is a message, and by fully embracing them, you can receive them. The answer you receive could be that you just need a good cry. Crying is a wonderful thing when done in the right amount of time. Stress Hormones are released in tears, which means you release stress as you cry. This letting go also creates emotional resilience. When you allow yourself to feel your emotions, you are less likely to get carried away by them.

Try embracing whatever you are feeling right now in this very moment. Sometimes we can't identify how we are feeling, and it can be confusing; however, the more you practice, the better you will get at it. Sit with your feelings and truly be with them as if they were your best friend trying to guide you. In this listening state, you can trust your gut, instinct, higher self, whatever you want to call it. Once you keep practicing, you cultivate a trust that you will know the answer within yourself. You will only know the answer once you sit with these feelings. It is the only way to transmute them. This is also a great time to ask yourself what you need. When you ask yourself what you need, you may resist doing what you internally know will make you feel better. Once you have listened to the message and the possible action associated, you will feel incredible.

Another great exercise is to ask yourself, "What am I meant to feel in this moment?" It may take some practice to hear the answer that truly serves you. However, the more you practice, the more you can listen and become deeply connected to your intuition.

This knowing is not the voice in your head but rather your deeper knowing. Your brain will be like on a hamster wheel if you start thinking about it. You instead feel it from your heart. Sit down and feel your heart and sit in your heart space. This is your notice to stop this dangerous cycle you may be stuck in by consistently running away from your feelings. The more you try to run away from them, the more imbalances show up, such as anxiety and panic attacks. If you start to feel off or at the beginning of anxiety, sit with your feelings to truly feel them so you may release them or transmute them. It is essential to listen to your body, especially when feeling off.

If you have not known how to handle your emotions, you are not alone. I used to bottle up all of my emotions. I had mini meltdowns where I would scream and cry, which would bring up racing thoughts about everything that had gone wrong with my life. I would then utilize the time to stuff the feelings back down. I would only express my feelings when the volume was turned up all the way. There was no way to ignore it. I did not let myself feel each feeling as they came. Instead, I pushed them down deep in my body, where they were stored. I stayed silent, thinking they would just go away, but they showed up later when I burst at the seams. I justified my position by saying I was a victim of some situation I had experienced. Even if I was the one who was "victimized," I still had the power to speak up. I still had the power to create an environment for my needs and wants to be met. I had way more influence over my emotional well-being than I gave myself credit for because I lived as a silent victim. Now, I turn my painful experiences into personal power and peace. You can do this, too, if you are willing to embark on the work that is necessary to accomplish such feats.

Embracing each emotion has allowed me to feel into my life fully. You may have times when you want to separate from the sadness because you are in a valley of your story. I instead found out that the best way to use sadness is to transform yourself. You can use your pain and create inner peace. Your pain could be the best thing that has ever happened to you. This mindset shift may seem radical, but it is so worth it.

When you do not deal with past traumas or stories you

tell yourself repeatedly, you can sometimes experience long-term low dose pain. You can use this time to face your darkest moments so that you may release this pain and rewrite these stories forever. How do you turn pain into peace? How do you make the hardships in your life the most healing experiences? You can use this opportunity to enrich your life. Your emotions are opportunities.

Once you master the embracing code, life will feel a little more effortless for you. Embracing your feelings and allowing them to come in enhances your ability to not be taken away by them at random times. Instead, you'll start to become emotionally intelligent and have emotional mastery.

EMBODIMENT PRACTICE

Embrace Exercises

1. Sit down and identify what you are feeling
    (anger, fear, pain, loneliness, jealousy,
    joy, gratitude, connection), then visualize
    yourself welcoming the feelings into your
    heart space like a friend that is here for
    you and you for them. You can create a
    mental image of a little cartoon character
    in your head or imagine a version of
    yourself experiencing this emotion. Hug
    this emotion and ask what this emotion is
    trying to tell you.

2. Sit down, identify what you are feeling, and ask yourself how to transmute this energy for your highest good. Embracing each emotion allows you to sit with yourself. Ask yourself, "(state your name), what do I need?"

CHAPTER 8

Enrich

Enhancing Your Life Through Your Emotions

THE SECOND STEP IN THE EMOTIONAL EXPRESSION journey is called "enrich." This is when you enrich your life using your emotions and the messages they bring. It is the process of fully feeling your feelings so that you may integrate the messages you receive. Not only do you want to embrace each emotion, but you also want to express it. This is where you get in a good cry or scream so that you can release the emotion and allow it to evolve. Letting yourself fully feel the emotion can be crucial to your well-being. You want to fully feel the happiness, fully feel the sadness, fully feel the gratitude, fully feel the anger so that you can enrich your life.

Enrichment is the process of enhancing the quality of your life and making it wealthier. These emotional processes will enrich and electrify your life because you will have chosen to. You are living in the human condition and are meant to experience all emotions. This is what it means to be alive. You are bringing life back into yourself as you let these feelings in. Then you can receive their messages. You must be open to receiving these messages so that you can go out and be a better version of yourself because of them.

A friend once said that she made herself feel sad, mad, or happy on command because she practiced eliciting these emotions. I thought this was a little crazy at first, and then I tried it and found it is a pretty effective trick. It is about emoting, or acting out all of your feelings so that they don't come back harder. Emotions are meant to be felt, and if you refuse to feel them, they will come back harder and threaten to drown you. Eliciting each emotion is a great way to create a loving relationship with anger, fear, jealousy, sadness, and happiness. If you are a little confused right now, here is an example: is there a song that you just can't listen to because it reminds you of a painful period of your life, a breakup, a death, etc.? Well, you can listen to it to elicit those feelings to come to the surface. You use it to feel sad or mad or a combination of both. You truly feel those emotions when you let them out in a safe environment. Then, listen to one of your favorite songs. This is an example of proactively exercising your emotional intelligence. Afterward, you may even feel relief when you realize that the song you could not listen to before no longer has power over you.

Emotions are meant to be felt. If you allow the "bad" feelings, then you may deeply feel the good ones because you are allowing yourself to be fully alive. Now you have the room to live vibrantly in every moment. As we let go of the past, we have more room for blessings now and in the future. By feeling your emotions, you are sending your future self some love. You hand your future self lighter and lighter baggage.

Enriching your life through emotions is about electrifying your life. It is about coming alive and waking up to the ecstasy that can be your life if you let it. Sometimes you can be your own worst enemy. How do I know this? Well, before I awoke to my new path, I was my own worst enemy. I was a slave to my painful toxic patterns that I had not released. I feel freedom beyond what I could have previously imagined because I allowed myself to become my best friend and cultivate loving relationships with myself, emotions, people, places, and experiences.

You may feel that any pain you endure is limiting your life. However, painful experiences can be your wake-up call to release all of the pain you have been carrying around for far too long and open yourself up to a world of possibilities. This moment is your opportunity to free yourself and no longer be a slave to your past heartaches.

Your feelings are also your fuel if you let them be. Let your feelings fuel you to be in action; let your emotions be a motivator in your journey. You manifest through the power of your emotions. You can enrich your life by manifesting the future you desire in the now.

You enrich your life through manifesting with emotions. First things first, what do you want to manifest? Knowing what you want is paramount to making it a reality and creating as much clarity as possible. If you want a vision to manifest, it can't be vague. I have learned the incredible power and magic of getting clear about exactly what you want. You have to say in great detail what that future is to you. Now I want you to write down what a future looks like if you embody health, vibrancy, and vitality. Who are you with? What are you doing? Use your senses. What does it smell like? What can you hear in this future of yours? What can you touch? What can you see? Close your eyes and bring in the vibrant colors. The most important part of envisioning what you desire is feeling what you want to feel. Bring in the emotions, and turn up the feelings as you continue to think about this vivacious future. Breathe it into every cell of your being.

Write down this crystal clear vision with the emotions associated. Then write down why you want to create this. Why do you want to live a full life? Why do you want to become the embodiment of health, vitality, and vibrancy? When you know your why, you have much more internal commitment to making this vision a reality.

After you have written down why you want your vision, ask yourself questions aloud. For example, you may ask, "What would it take for me to accomplish this vision?" You may also ask "how" questions. Asking "how" questions aloud allows your brain to start searching for the answers; you do not need to have any answers yet. Some examples of these questions that you say out loud are: what would it take for me to be physically healthy? How can I get mentally healthy? What would it take to be emotionally healthy? How can I allow myself to be spiritually healthy? Remember, you do not need to know the answers. Just asking the right questions to yourself can be magical in your life because the messages will start to flood in. However, you must take action when you receive these answers and continue to be in aligned action.

Using your emotions to enrich your life allows you to choose that vision and make your health non-negotiable. Your future is in your hands; where do you want to go, why do you want to be there, and how do you want to show up for yourself? It is all your choice. Making conscious and intentional choices toward your vision is essential to achieving the health you desire. When you wield your emotional powers, you will be astonished at the accelerated results that follow.

I remember reading my first manifestation journal months later, and my breath was taken away. As I used my emotions as my fuel, my opportunity to enrich my life, I realized that I had manifested everything I had set out to create. I sat there in tears of gratitude because I made that happen for myself. I had read all the things I had written down, and I was astonished because I couldn't believe how things were starting to turn out. I showed up for myself, and it was more than I possibly could have imagined. Another integration to this method that I now like to use is after visualizing or writing down what I desire, I say, "This or better." I allow all that I don't know yet I am capable of achieving into my reality. I am open to receiving. However,

I was not always open to these blessings. When I had no real relationship to my emotions, I had no stability to call in the reality I desired. I was always waiting for whatever I wanted to come into form without dancing with the process. I was looking for happiness to come through from my manifestation instead of coming from me.

I find it so funny that we all have a goal of being happy. Have you asked yourself what makes you deeply happy and fulfilled? Find something that brings you pure, innocent joy and self-love and integrate it into your life. There is an abundance of ways to integrate this into your reality. True fulfillment in life comes from within, from your dance with receiving love. Love of ourselves, the people in our lives, nature, our passions, etc.

You have a choice to be empathetic to yourself. You may hear things such as love yourself more and get rid of your stress. What does that actually look like? What are the tools and strategies to achieve these great heights? Well, I found that if you want to evolve yourself to the next, best version of yourself, daily practices of forgiveness, gratitude, and self-love are key.

EMBODIMENT PRACTICE

Use your emotions to create the life you desire

1. Write down the future in great detail, including sensory feelings (see, smell, touch, hear, taste).

2. Write down what you are doing and who you are with.

3. Write down what you want to feel in this future.

4. Here, visualize the future you desire with crystal clarity. Feel the emotions.

5. Imagine that you are turning up a dial that turns up the feelings in your body. Do it until you are now bursting with that feeling.

6. Know in your heart that what you desire will come true.

CHAPTER 9

Evolve

Transformational Practices to Become a Better Version of You

EVOLVING IS WHERE YOU CAN PUT SOME GREAT TRAN-scendental practices to work for you so that you may heal daily. They are essential to my day, and I am sure you will not want to stop when you start seeing the results that these practices can have on your life. It might be tempting to stop because you are in a "good place mentally." However, these transcendental practices are muscles you work on, and you do not want to let them atrophy. These practices are like going to the gym for emotional wellness, inner peace, and freedom. Forgiveness is a beautiful place to start to make room for more transformations to occur.

FORGIVENESS

I always thought that I had forgiven someone when I was still holding that negative charge within myself. I would say, "I forgive you," and I wouldn't mean it. I wanted to forgive them, but I didn't know how. Forgiveness is the number one important factor when truly moving on with your life, but it can be the most difficult thing to do. It took me a very long time to forgive others in my past. Forgiveness to yourself is the absolute key. It is the weight that gets lifted off your shoulders that you didn't even realize you were carrying around. This is called liberation. Once you are unshackled from your past, you are truly free. This, again, is no easy feat and takes a lot of intention. Forgiveness for yourself and or others can be a daily practice, and it will take a little while to fully appreciate the incredible effects.

Forgiveness is a process, and there are layers. Some say maybe you will need to do a forgiveness exercise for a few days or weeks. I needed to do them for months, maybe even years, to truly forgive. I used to think, "Maybe I am just stubborn, or I let my feelings fester for too long." Do not judge yourself for how long this takes. With each layer, you begin to forgive deeper and deeper. This is not a black or white process. At least it wasn't for me.

Suppose you are having a really hard time forgiving someone or even yourself or both. A nightly chant can be useful. You might say, "I forgive ____, and I wish them happiness, peace, love, and everything their heart desires." It will be hard to say at first. I remember feeling so confused when I spoke this phrase out loud. There was a part of me that wanted to offer well wishes to those I wanted to forgive, but the tinge of hurt and sorrow was still there. I felt deeply hurt and betrayed. But you must keep saying it until you believe it. Eventually, you will. When I started to forgive through this mantra, I was able to breathe easier and felt that my heart was no longer breaking when I thought of the people I wanted to forgive. Forgiveness is a deeply spiritual practice. Why did I put it in the emotional category? Forgiveness is an evolution of your emotions and allows you to greatly evolve in your life and walk into your highest timeline.

Forgiveness for yourself is first and foremost. I have learned a practice to integrate into my daily routine. Sometimes I forgive myself for the little mishaps or slips of the tongue, and I frequently forgive myself for my mistakes. The key to forgiveness is to register what you have learned from this experience. Once you can articulate what you have learned, you can let go of the pain. It might not be right away, but once you make different choices in your life, you are free from reliving the lesson over and over again. Your life will drastically change. Life will not have to get louder and louder with the same lesson if you take action to make new choices that serve you by integrating the message.

Now, this type of work did not seem to be important at first but again has the potential to change your life experience. Think of the residual negative charges towards other people, events, and situations. It is time to practice releasing them through a forgiveness exercise.

During a forgiveness exercise,

o   Remember the event or person you want to
    forgive (and be specific; your words hold so
    much power when you practice clarity in
    what you are forgiving).

    •   Embrace the emotions to come, and
        allow a safe space for yourself.

o   Feel the pain they or it caused you (for only a
    few seconds).

    •   Enrich and truly feel these feelings so
        that you may let go.

o   See it from their eyes so that you may

understand and forgive.

- Evolve. There is a place where forgiveness is not needed because you instead understand.

o Name something you have learned from this event.

- This will help you move past and maybe even feel grateful for the lesson that this person or event has given you.

- If they are a family member or someone in your life that you love but could not express your needs to, now is the time to start setting boundaries and expressing your needs so that you do not have to forgive this person or yourself repeatedly.

o Imagine giving the person or event a hug.

- If you can imagine yourself hugging them, you probably have a great grasp on forgiving them.

- Imagine that they are your child. What compassion would you give them? What level of unconditional

> love and forgiveness would you
> exercise?

o Watch the person, place, situation, etc.
   disappear and feel yourself release the hurt

In forgiveness, you can recognize that people don't just do actions for nothing. Trying to see the event from the person that wronged you, which can be hard, even if it is yourself. I know that the number one person I needed to forgive the most was myself. I realized that similar situations and people were repeatedly hurting me because I allowed myself to be hurt by them. I was not active when it came to my health. I acted like a victim for so long. I allowed stories and beliefs to limit me. This was the tip of the iceberg; however, forgiving myself was liberating. I was able to create a deeper relationship with myself through this transformational practice. I also rebuilt trust with myself because I knew I would take different actions from then on. Once you can master this skill, you will be able to forgive faster and let go of the negative charges from your past and present. You then have the opportunity to feel gratitude towards these situations or people. Forgiveness for yourself and others will allow you to lead with more love, compassion, joy, and gratitude.

EMBODIMENT PRACTICE

Use this forgiveness statement:

I forgive _____, and I wish them happiness, peace,
love, and everything their heart desires. Say it
both out loud and write it down if you need to.
Use this statement daily until you forgive fully
and deeply believe what you are saying.

GRATITUDE

Gratitude is extremely important for the mind, body, and soul. Gratitude is a seed of transformation, growth, and vibrancy. When you become grateful, more blessings start coming into your life because you become the vibration of magnetizing good fortune and opportunity. Being grateful for what you have allows you to vibrantly live in the here and now and opens you up to a future full of blessings. It is a commonality in our society to take things for granted because we do not have conscious time for gratitude. Think about how you were able to read this book right now. You can read it and comprehend the language it is in. That is an incredible skill and blessing, yet something that we often take for granted.

Have you ever done something for someone else and felt that you had been taken for granted? You feel that you give and you give and you have not been acknowledged. This is the time to acknowledge yourself. You can show gratitude to yourself and appreciate all that you do. When I was first introduced to this idea, I felt a little uncomfortable. Isn't that a little conceited? I have learned that it is not conceited at all because if you acknowledge yourself, you are not waiting for people in your life to do it, which helps keep your relationships healthy. Also, if you are grateful for yourself, you allow the people in your life to give you recognition. Doesn't that sound counterintuitive? Well, it's not because if you recognize and appreciate yourself, you believe you deserve the accolades. Many people are desperate for acknowledgment and appreciation, but it feels so foreign to them that they can't accept it when they hear it. Here is an example to illustrate this concept.

You do something for someone

Them: "Thank you so much for doing x,y, and z."

You: "It is no problem; there is no need to thank me."

Have you ever done this? I know I have. You teach others how to treat you. If you consistently say that it is no problem and or there is no need to thank you, you are teaching people not to appreciate you. You have communicated that you are superhuman and do not need acknowledgment. This is the power of word choice because they will believe you. Those words you spoke go straight into their mind, that you do not need acknowledgment and that the task(s) was not a great effort on your part. Maybe the next time you do something similar for that person, and you don't get thanked. You may say, "What a jerk!" In reality, you told them to treat you this way.

I have victimized myself in this way. For many years I did not realize it. Now, I say, "You are very welcome," or "I do it because I love you." I acknowledge myself first so that I know I am worthy of accepting gratitude from others. I have seen many people get stuck on receiving gratitude, even from themselves, because they want to be a nice and humble person who doesn't need appreciation. But how are you a genuinely nice person if you are not nice to yourself? At that point, you are just creating a facade, a mask to hide how you are secretly subtly abusing yourself by not allowing yourself appreciation or self-gratitude. This ideology may seem harsh, but once you start giving yourself the love and appreciation you deserve, you will be amazed at all you have taken away from your life by holding back your ability to receive.

There are different techniques for intentional gratitude. The most common and intentional practice is having a gratitude journal be a part of your morning or night routine. This allows you to either start or end your day in gratitude. I particularly like practicing intentional gratitude right before bed, but that is just a preference. Another way to practice gratitude is by programming it into your subconscious mind through affirmations, hypnosis, etc. I have programmed myself so that my first thought in the morning is, "Thank you for this new day, for this new opportunity, thank you for the present that is today that I get to unwrap." I used to snooze my alarm for hours at a time, and now I jump out of bed, excited for the day.

Another incredible thing about gratitude is that it can actually change the structure of a collection of atoms. A scientist named Dr. Emoto looked at water and said certain phrases to it. One of the phrases was "you disgust me," which caused the water molecules to transform into a terrible, ugly mess. One of the other phrases was "thank you," which also changed the particles under a microscope. They went from a disarrayed mess to what looked like a beautiful snowflake. When I first saw this, I was mesmerized[39]. How could it be? The words you speak to water change its molecular structure in a scientifically measurable way. What mystics, gurus, and healers have said throughout the centuries is showing to be more and more provable. If you are largely made up of water, saying things such as "you disgust me" could be changing yourself molecularly. Similarly, by saying "thank you" to yourself possibly you can be changing the structure within your body.

Your body especially deserves your gratitude. Your body is constantly working towards health and vitality. It is protecting you, loving you, and keeping you in balance in this very second. Give it the love and support and gratitude it deserves. The more you can connect with your body, the more you will be grounded, present, and able to flourish in all aspects of life.

EMBODIMENT
PRACTICE

*Right now, write down 100
things that you are truly grateful
for. Close your eyes and take a
breath of gratitude for each item
you write.*

SELF-LOVE

Self-love is when you give yourself permission to be loved. It is radically accepting who you are and all parts of you. It is committing to a journey of transformation and being devoted to your mind, body, and soul. There are an infinite number of ways for you to practice self-love. The ones that people often think of are taking a bath, taking a nap, or resting. All are fantastic practices of love, but they represent surface-level self-love. However, there is a deeper form of self-love that is transcendent. The one where you become the hero of your life, where you are so loving to yourself that love just pours out of you, where you deeply are connected to yourself, where you feel the magic of life because you are enchanted by yourself and your own love.

The most important first step to cultivating a deeply loving relationship with yourself and incorporating practices of self-love is to give yourself permission to love yourself. Knowing that you are enough is often the hardest part. You have always been enough, and you will always be enough. Throughout our lives, we are shown "proof" that we are not enough when we are not perfect. There may have been a time in your life when you learned to think that you are not good enough. Maybe a parent made you feel like you weren't enough, maybe an event made you feel like you weren't enough. Whatever the situation may be, I am here to tell you that you are completely enough, but it is up to you to fully accept that truth.

Repeat in your head or aloud, right here and right now, "I am enough. I have always been enough, and I will always be enough."

The next step towards the journey to self is accepting all parts of you. This acceptance comes with practice and is exercised with awareness. The more you become aware of your inner workings, the more you can radically accept yourself. You deserve to love all parts of yourself, which starts with acceptance of self. Once you give yourself the love and acceptance you have been searching for, your life will change forever. If there is one promise I can make in this book, it's that unconditional love for yourself is a magical process. It creates positive waves throughout your entire life.

There are huge differences between conditional and unconditional love. Loving yourself conditionally can be very dangerous. If you love yourself conditionally, you will only give that love if, for example, you become successful or if you are in a relationship. This way of living is extremely dangerous because love is not supposed to be conditional. If you love from a conditional standpoint, you are coming from a place of lack. You don't have enough love in your life, so if x,y, or z doesn't happen, you are stuck without love. Once you discover true unconditional self-love in your life, ripples of blessings will unfold. Once you start accepting yourself, it won't matter if someone else is having a bad day and isn't showing you the love you deserve. You deserve unconditional love, and you deserved it yesterday. You can tap into it right now.

Not only is accepting yourself extremely important, it is also imperative that you accept your past self and project love to your future self. Accepting your life just as it is and loving it can be a grueling task. We have not been taught this practice of acceptance in our society, but once you start doing it, you can be liberated from the shackles of resisting your reality. You may wonder why you didn't start until now. We often judge our past selves for our mistakes and failures. However, if it weren't for those experiences and the lessons you learned, you would not be the beautiful person that you are today. This idea does not mean that you do not strive to improve. Self-love and acceptance is a journey and not a destination. Self-love and acceptance are things you have to practice as you grow, transform, and heal.

You can significantly enhance your self-acceptance by searching for parts of yourself that you do not like. This may seem counterintuitive but bear with me. Think of something that you judge about yourself. Now I want you to imagine this version of you that purely presents that quality you do not like standing in front of you. This is when visualization or intention of love can be extremely powerful. You can send a loving light or a hug to the part that you identified. You can even send love to the judge within you. When you send love to parts of yourself that you do not like, you become more whole. Accepting yourself is about becoming more whole because you bring together all pieces of you with love.

Accepting yourself leads you to a place where you can nurture a connection to yourself. One of my favorite ways to cultivate my connection to self is through mirror work. To practice this method, go to the mirror and look yourself straight in the eye. At first, this is an uncomfortable practice for many because you may have never given yourself attention like this before. Try staring into your own eyes for at least five minutes. A deeper form of this exercise is when you put the mirror close to your face to look only into one eye. A little handheld mirror might make this deeper form of the exercise easier. The mirror needs to be close to your face to look deeply into your own eye. The eyes are the windows to the soul, and when we stare into our own eyes, we deeply connect to who we truly are.

Did you know that one study found that eye contact is extremely important in creating a deep bond[40]? Well, It is time you deeply bond with yourself. If you can fall in love with yourself, your whole life will be different because more of your expressions of love become magical.

You can also practice this exercise by looking into the mirror, saying your name out loud, creating an intention of a safe space, telling yourself what you forgive yourself for, and telling yourself what you are thankful for and what you love about yourself.

This is a very powerful exercise. For you, it may seem so foreign to be with yourself. More often than not, we don't sit with ourselves and say these things. We usually do not tell ourselves that we love aspects of who we are and how we live life; we do not usually speak out loud that we forgive ourselves. I will bet that the biggest critic in your life is yourself. How do I know that? Well, that is my biggest critic. Even forgiving myself for being critical of myself is extremely freeing. It may feel more comfortable and familiar to be against yourself. Even though creating a connection to self may not feel familiar, it will serve you and your fullest potential of living a vivacious life.

Mirror work has been a crucial tool in creating a deeply

loving relationship with myself. This is not something I did once or did for some time. Rather, it is a practice I have committed to. I love connecting with myself in this way because I give myself the attention I deserve and desire. It allows me to be unapologetically loving; it allows me to deeply connect to self and to have a space to heal, transform and embody love itself. There is something extremely special about being with yourself in this way and committing to the practice of being with self.

Self-commitment is key if you want to live as a vibrant embodiment of love. It is a beautiful expression of love. Once you are completely devoted to the well-being of your mind, body, and soul, you can love at a transcendental level. You deserve to give yourself all of this love consistently. Every action you take in one day can be an act of devotion to self, an intention of love, and a conscious decision.

One of the most imperative ways of practicing self-love is by making every action you take a devotion to self. I tell my clients that days of devotion are a great conscious and intentional way to start practicing this. A day of devotion is a day you reserve in your calendar, like a date you have with yourself. During this day, every single thing you do is in devotion to yourself and your well-being. This idea might scare some people. They might immediately say, "Oh, I can't do that. I have too much going on, I don't have time, I have responsibilities." Believe me, your brain is creating these thoughts because it is scary to make such a change in your life. Work through this resistance. Reserve one day out of a month or a week to give yourself this gift. If you are confused about what that day would look like, ask yourself, "What are the ways that I am searching for love in my life, and how can I give that to myself?"

In this moment, remember things that you have done for others in any type of relationship. Have you written someone a long sappy love letter or text before? One of the most profound ways that I have found to express love to self is by writing a love letter, and yes, this letter can be long, romantic, and sappy. How would you talk to yourself if you were deeply in love with yourself, and how can you show up in this way?

If you are still confused about what to do during this day of devotion to self, start to ask yourself more questions. How do you show up for your friends, family, significant others, and kids? What are the little things you do daily, weekly, monthly, and yearly to show your love for them? What are ways that you show and express love?

Now how do you show love to yourself? Do you show

up for yourself the same way you show up for others? Can you do the same for yourself as a way of practicing devotion to yourself?

Practicing deep self-love is essential to your life because when you look for happiness and love from outside yourself, it is a hit or miss. From my experience, most of us have expectations of outside love. When those expectations are not met, the hurt we experience is immense. We are subconsciously taught to seek approval, appreciation, and acceptance from family, friends, society, partners, etc. These are normal feelings, but everything changed for me when I realized that I wasn't allowing people in because of the way I was showing up. I wasn't allowing them to fully love me because I was not fully loving myself. I wasn't allowing myself to receive their love because I wasn't giving myself permission to do so, and I held deep-seated beliefs that I was not worthy. I was the one holding me back. Having loving relationships with others first needs to come from the inside so that you can then accept love from others and share your love without restriction. Your love is meant to be free and ever-expanding. This process is going to feel weird at first if you are in the habit of self-rejection or avoidance. I know because that is how I felt. It was so strange to show myself love, but it was magical. Once you break through those barriers of resistance, love will feel freeing and abundant, and you will have access to an everlasting well of love from within.

EMBODIMENT PRACTICE

Play with mirror work in any form that feels right to you.

1. Just be with yourself as you look into the mirror and say, "I am here for you."
2. Look into one of your eyes for one to five minutes.

3. Use transformational practices as you look into your eyes in a mirror and say out loud:

- *Your name, I forgive you for X3*

- *Your name, I am grateful to you because... X3*

- *Your name, I am in awe of you because... X3*

BRINGING THE THREE E'S TOGETHER

EMBODYING EMOTIONAL HEALTH SEEMS EASY TO PEO-
ple when they hear the exercises. However, they usually
do not implement them because they have such resistance
to doing them. Connecting deeply to your emotions is so
imperative for you to live the reality you desire. Through
embracing your emotions, you deeply connect with them.
You provide a safe space for you to feel them fully and to
receive the messages from those feelings. When you practice enrichment, you enhance your life through the power
of your emotions. You manifest from your emotions and
take action on the messages that you receive. You also practice emotional intelligence by fully feeling the different
emotions you elicit. Through transformational practices,
you evolve yourself greatly. Forgiveness, gratitude, and self-
love will come in handy in any situation or experience life
has to offer you.

Happiness can be effortless to some and fleeting to others. If you ask people what they want out of life, they might say they want to be happy, but do they have a clear vision of what that looks like? It is quite impossible to be happy 24/7. This is coming from a person that others perceive and label as a happy person. However, I, too, am a complex being who needs to express my emotions. Our different combinations of emotions each day create a masterpiece of art. All of your emotions and experiences throughout the day are strokes on this beautiful complex canvas. By embracing each emotion, we can release and move on to the next to create the full picture. We all go through cycles in our lives where there are many peaks and valleys. In our peaks, we lean on the happy side, but we still feel every emotion. What does happiness mean to you? Define it so that you can go get it.

These may seem like easy actions, but you may meet them with a lot of resistance. Remember that there is no emotionally healthy destination. Instead, you must practice. Consistency may be the most challenging aspect of this journey. Your mind might tell you that you don't need to practice right now when, more often than not, now is the exact time to practice connecting to your emotions. You owe it to yourself to start practicing now because that is when real results will shine through.

I have made these excuses, and sometimes I still struggle with getting myself to practice. That is why creating new habits that serve you and committing to yourself is the key. I am proactive in my life so that if something comes my way to throw me off-balance, I will come back to balance quicker because I already have the tools in place.

PART IV
Embodying Vibrant
Spiritual Health

THE POWER OF
YOUR SPIRITUALITY

SPIRITUALITY IS NOT JUST A PLACE TO FIND TOOLS TO allow us to come back into balance; it is the sturdy foundation for many that allow the balance to happen in the first place. Spirituality is a beautiful part of life where exploration is abundant. I give myself permission to change my mind, to expand, and to be fluid when it comes to my journey in the valley of spirituality. I invite you to give yourself permission to explore. When it comes to choosing my spiritual beliefs, I ask myself, "If everything is a dream, if life is a dream, if none of our reality is really 'real,' what would be the most empowering belief to embody?" I survey each belief as if I get to choose what I believe to be true. For each belief I ask, does this belief serve me, make me a better person, or make my life better? If the answer is yes, then I allow myself to believe. Maybe that belief will change or maybe it won't but feeling the freedom to choose beliefs is truly empowering.

People get really angry at each other when they have differing beliefs. There is a lot of turmoil in this area because people try to push others to believe in what they believe. I do not subscribe to this practice, as it creates relationships to spirituality that are founded on turmoil and resistance. Many people do not want to explore this area because they feel pushed. Or they may belong to a religion and do not want to allow themselves to look at others' practices or even appreciate them because it is not part of their belief system. If you are feeling resistance, I understand. I invite you to explore your beliefs and survey your beliefs, and if they are still ones that you want to keep, that is amazing. In that case, you are consciously choosing your beliefs, which is incredible. Many people do not do this. Most of us belong to the religion of our parents or avoid religion because of our parents without ever stopping to consciously choose to have faith or create a personal connection to God.

There is usually a moment that allows you to realize the power of spiritual paths. Notice how I say paths; there is no right or wrong way to explore. You are allowed to try things or practices that might not serve you at first. You are allowed to change your mind, get into deeper forms of practice, etc. It is the adventure inwards, finding what you believe, having faith in that belief, and using spirituality as a part of your life that enlivens you.

I knew my spiritual journey was truly serving me when my nightmares started to become empowering and spiritual experiences. During the very painful period of my life, I was plagued with nightly nightmares. I would wake up terrified and paralyzed. When these dreams started to become empowering, I woke up feeling like I could do anything and be anyone.

I hold one of these dreams dear to my heart because it showed me how my spiritual exploration was empowering me to face the darkness within. In this dream, I was in my kitchen, and the lights were all off. The darkness was palpable, and eeriness crept through my entire body. I stood there, unsure of what was going to happen, but my stomach was trembling, and my eyes were wide open. Blinking didn't seem like a safe option. That is when I saw it—the dark, shadow-like figure floating. It looked like a combination of a Harry Potter dementor and an ancient widow as it had a dark veil over its facelessness. It floated in front of me. I didn't want to move for fear that it would not notice me. I watched as it walked from the kitchen down my stairs to the lower floor. I was thinking, "What do I do? What if it comes back up the stairs?" I watched the stairs, my heart racing, completely frozen. Then I saw it again.

The figure started coming up the stairs at full speed toward me. For a brief moment, I had no idea what to do. Then this strength started to burst through me. I opened my arms wide, and I said out loud, "I am love, I am light, I am divinely protected." Light started shining from my body, and the light transformed the dark shadow figure into a version of myself that was crying. I comforted that version of myself until I woke up.

This dream showed me that I was transmuting the dark and using it to comfort parts of myself that I had long abandoned. I love to analyze dreams. I do it almost every morning to see how my subconscious is processing. This dream had a whole lot of meaning. First, this dream showed me I was ignoring parts of myself that were hurt and needed my attention, affection, and love. I learned that those dark, scary things are not scary when light and truth are shined on them. The part that struck me the most was that I turned a nightmare into an empowering dream and one of faith. That is when I knew I had started my journey to true unshakable faith. I woke up feeling so peaceful, protected, and loved. I was so proud that I had made changes in my conscious mind and significant changes in my subconscious mind. I started having more dreams that started as nightmares. I would just say, "I am light, I am light, I am divinely protected," and light would shine from me until whatever seemed dark transformed into the truth. Each time this dream repeated in a new scenario, and I woke up empowered.

Having a connection to your spirit is not like any other experience on the planet. It is filled with this inner knowing that can help you with direction in your life. It can help you make decisions; it can help you know what serves you and what doesn't. It can tell you what is truth and what is an illusion. Having a connection to your spirit gives you an empowered self that is unshakable, a self that is in safety, a self that is grounded, a self that is filled with endless love, a self that allows you to surrender, a self that allows for the practice of radical acceptance. When you connect deeply to your spirit, you unlock a knowing within yourself that has been there all along. Having a connection to spirit is when you truly experience the Divine. It is more profound than simply practicing religion. Having a connection to your spirit allows you to be in touch with your energy body and the energy that fills this beautiful world and beyond. Go ahead and take a moment here to breathe as you feel into your spirit. Even if you can't quite feel it, that is okay; just know it is there.

You will see that I use many names for higher power,

such as God, The Universe, Divine Love, The Infinite, etc. For me, these are just words that mean the same thing. Just like how other languages have words associated with a higher power, there are different ways to describe the same thing for me, though I do not force this idea on you. The beauty is that you get to decide if this is true for you.

Finding this belief in Divine Love enables you a key to a foundation of vibrancy and resiliency, the feeling of safety. Having faith in something unlocks the potential for enhancing your well-being. It does not matter if you do not want to use terms such as a God or a Higher Power or Universe. Having faith in life and knowing that life has your back can give you a sturdy foundation.

EMBODIMENT
PRACTICE

Give yourself permission to explore.

Write down or say aloud, "I give myself permission to explore my spirituality."

CHAPTER 10

Safety

Trusting in Yourself, Your Life and Your Higher Power

SAFETY IS DEFINED IN THIS CONTEXT AS HAVING A deep, unshakable knowing that you can trust yourself, your life, and your higher power. Knowing that there is a higher being that is benevolent is the epitome of extreme comfort. I believe that we all want to search for this Divine Love, but many of us are too scared to start genuinely searching because we know that we will find it. There is a difference between hearing about God and experiencing it. These can be extremely personal experiences, but I invite you to explore.

If you feel an internal battle is preventing you from exploring this topic, I understand. I grew up as a Catholic, and my father tried to counter those teachings with some of the other religions, such as Buddhism or different philosophies. I had one parent who loved and found comfort in religion and one who despised the existence of organized religions as there have been many wars waged because of them. I struggled for a very long time to discover what I believed and have that integrated into my life. I think it is important to see where I was because you may be there too. I grew up in CCD (Catholic Sunday School). I found church boring as a kid, which is very understandable. I knew my father had such an issue with Catholicism because of the excuses people made in the name of God. I also came to that understanding as I learned more in school. I also learned about the connections in the different religions and how they are all really the same at the core, interconnected in many ways, and built off of one another. I was confused for many years about my beliefs. I would pray without feeling it, or I would pray when things were going really bad in my life. I wouldn't know who I was talking to; I would just be begging for mercy. I went through an internal battle because I did not like much of the oppression or manipulation that many religions used to coerce people into doing what they wanted to do. I also felt this deep desire to connect to a higher power, feel safe, and unlock the faith inside me that I didn't know how to tap into.

I did not know what I believed in. As I started to be conscious and ask myself what I believed, I had to go looking for some answers. I invite you to take this journey by asking yourself what you believe in, why you believe in it, and whether it is beneficial to you. Sometimes we see religion and the people in it, and we put all those who believe in God in this box of this experience that you may have had. I always felt a little weird, as if I did not belong in the religious or spiritual spaces. Because of my permission to explore, I am now happy to go to any institution and try out their practices. It becomes a beautiful exploration, and I am safe in what I believe. If someone tries to tell me I am wrong or that I need to stick to a dogma or something of that nature, I am grounded in the safety of my beliefs. I also highly respect everyone in every religion because I believe that they are all the same, just using different terminology and stories to understand The Infinite.

Exploring different terms for God helped me transcend all of the noise that was religion. It was my pathway to freedom of spirituality. I could see through the parts of other spiritual paths or religious paths that did not serve me. Now I feel safe using the term God because I allowed myself to explore. This safe space you are creating is using love as the fabric, and you are allowed to make this experience your own.

Another part of spiritual exploration that helped me transcend the noise of others' beliefs was when I learned the difference in "prayer" or aligning my vibration to what I desired. There have been many different ways to "pray" or manifest that have been presented to me. Two of my favorites are as follows. One way is to tell God that you are faithful and surrender to grace. This is the ultimate form of unshakable faith. There is no need to ask for anything because you know it will be okay. The other form is thanking the universe for what it has already given you and all it will give you. This comes from a vibration of love and gratitude. Through this practice, I got to know deep in my soul that everything is meant to be and will be. As I was taught in my life, some people pray with the feeling of fear in their hearts. If we pray with fear, that is the feeling we attract. Our words and thoughts are taken very literally. We receive exactly what we say and feel. Gratitude and faith allow blessings into our lives. Being grateful and having faith elevates your frequency so that you become a magnet to all that God wants to gift you. When I went from "please God help me" to "thank you God for these blessings," a radical shift in my relationship with spirit formed. I used to only pray or connect to my Spiritual Guides when I needed help. However, creating a relationship with the infinite allowed me to pray in a way that serves me. There is a huge difference between begging for mercy and practicing faith.

When I started to pray, I was able to tap into this infinite well of love from within and without. Again, nothing can describe this experience in its entirety until you experience it yourself. I invite you just to give yourself permission to try. It is like falling in love; you don't know what the experience is like until it happens to you, and it can be difficult to explain it to someone who has not experienced it. There is something so special about having that real connection to God, to spirit. When you permit yourself to have this faith, this foundation, and to connect with infinite love in this way, you unlock a new dimension of life. I am not telling you what to do; instead, I am inviting you to a beautiful experience.

If you keep unlocking the safety code, you may recognize the power of faith. This invitation is only a proposition to enhance your life and not a direct assignment. I used to hate when people tried to shove religion or spirituality down my throat. After going through this journey,

I feel that I have more of an understanding of why people try to convert you to their religion in public places. They probably had an experience where they felt that they were saved by God or their religion. I can understand, as my whole life changed for the better because of my spiritual exploration. This journey is an inward one, and one cannot force another to believe in anything.

I invite you to feel into the safety in your life. Feeling safe even in your own body allows you to listen and follow your intuition. Now is the time to listen to your inner knowing because that is where you will find safety. If you listen to that inner feeling, it will steer you in the right direction.

EMBODIMENT
PRACTICE

Ask yourself:

1. What do I believe, and does that belief serves me?
2. Do I have faith in myself, my life, and my higher power?
3. What can I do to have unshakable faith in one of these areas?
4. Do I feel safe in my beliefs?

CHAPTER 11

Surrender

Practicing Radical Acceptance

SURRENDER IS ACCEPTING EVERYTHING AS IT IS EX-actly as it is. It is about self-acceptance first and foremost. If you are in complete surrender mode, so much beauty can happen in your life and in so many ways. Surrender is having complete acceptance for the moment, how people are, and how your situation may be. Surrender is a place where you accept what feels unacceptable. From this place, you learn to love yourself and others in a much more un-conditional space. When you completely let go of how things are supposed to be, you realize everything is as it should be. Sometimes it may be uncomfortable, but this moment can bring so much inner peace. This peace allows your body, mind, and soul to heal at a deeper level.

Surrender is about cultivating this peace through this acceptance. This isn't to say that you do not do everything in your power to create the life that you deserve. I trust that you can see just how powerful you are. Evening wielding the ability to practice surrender is your internal way of creating inner peace. You have the power to create serenity for yourself. Inner peace is when you truly feel in alignment with the world around you. Giving yourself to the moment with love is powerful. You feel that you are in the right place at the right time, and you become timeless. This is where the true gold of life is. This is where your awakening is. Everything can change for you when you start to have this awareness.

An awakening makes you more open and accepting of life as it is, not as you want it to be. The situations you want to ignore, that you are so desperately hoping and wishing to go away, are your gifts. Surrender is about fully embracing these gifts.

Sometimes pain can be our greatest motivator to a spiritual awakening and complete surrender and radical acceptance of what is. Suffering so deeply, where your body is in disease, your heart is utterly broken, or your soul is shattered, is when you wake up to the truth. The truth is that you do not have to suffer. Pain is something that will continue to come into our lives, but we never have to suffer through it.

Surrender is about experiencing everything through a new lens. You can experience your life through observation, acceptance, and unconditional love. This is not about optimism or even looking at everything in a positive light. That is not the goal. Instead, this perspective is about radical self-acceptance and acceptance of everything around you. It is a place where you remember that nothing is separate from you, and you look at everything with love. It is not about labeling anything as good or bad; it just is. Yes, there are times to be sad, mad, and in pain, but you do not need to live from pain.

Surrender is allowing everything to be exactly as it is, accepting the moment as it is. The act of surrendering does not mean giving up. Once you're able to completely surrender to your circumstances, you have the true power to change them because you are no longer desperate. You use different energy when you have an unentangled mindset. We can design our reality through creativity with no expectation. Surrender is also synonymous in this context with new states of consciousness or new states of awareness.

A spiritual experience I hold dear to my heart is one that felt like an immersion into surrender. I was sitting and reading *The Power of Now* by Eckhart Tolle[41], and I came across a passage that read, "The reason why some people love to engage in dangerous activities, such as mountain, climbing, car racing, and so on, although they may not be aware of it, is that it forces them into the Now—that intensely alive state that is free of time, free of problems, free of thinking, free of the burden of the personality. Slipping away from the present moment even for a second may mean death. Unfortunately, they come to depend on a particular activity to be in that state. But you do not need to climb the north face of the Eiger. You can enter that state now." I can't explain what happened, but my body was flooded with this bliss state. I felt I had been immersed into unconditional love that surrounded me and was within me. I felt very still and intensely in the moment. I sat there in complete bliss. I did not feel I needed to do anything or be anyone. I felt that I was just observing everything and deeply believing that everything was just the way it was supposed to be at that moment. It felt that I was in a space where unshakable faith and safety were born. I sat there for hours, observing this beautiful conscious awareness.

If these conscious processes bring up some fear for you, that is fantastic, because it means that you are going to change or transform in some way that serves you. However, to remedy some of this fear in this moment, practice surrendering daily. Sleep is another way of surrendering daily and is a vital part of your journey and so are the messages in your dreams. Sleep is when your body is healed and restored. More specifically, it has been said that when you are in the deepest sleep or the delta state of mind, you are being cleansed by the Divine Spirit. This process is about being a part of the "one," or the infinite energy. You can tap into this energy both consciously and unconsciously. You can believe in this phenomenon or not. It is up to you to decide. However, the practice of surrendering benefits you whether you believe in a higher power or not.

Surrender is about allowing everything to be exactly as it is. You are not doing anything but being. This is a beautiful state to be in, and I invite you to explore how you can be living in being rather than doing.

EMBODIMENT PRACTICE

1. Find a comfortable seat.

2. Take a deep, conscious breath in.

3. Start to listen to the silence around you. Silence has a distinct fabric that you can hear. When you tune into silence, you open yourself up to the nothingness and the infinity that is this moment.

4. Become aware of all of your senses all at once.

CHAPTER 12

Serenity

Playing with Your Energy

SERENITY IS UTILIZING ENERGY WORK. WHEN I FIRST started practicing energy medicine, I was doing it because I was in physical pain and willing to try anything. As I started to use it regularly, I realized that it was a much more helpful and profound practice than I ever could have imagined. At first, I couldn't feel anything, but now when I do energy medicine, I feel deeply connected to my energy body. It feels like I am cleansing my body inside and out. As I got more comfortable with trying out different forms of energy medicine, I started doing weird hand and body movements following my intuition when I got into a meditative state. I felt self-conscious while doing the practice, even though no one was watching. I then remembered my commitment to myself, and that it was my duty to try absolutely everything that was meant to help me heal. I let go and let my inner knowing take over, even when I felt a little uncomfortable with it. Your inner intelligence already knows what you need to do to help you, but you need to first listen to it and surrender to the unknown.

During the very beginning of my journey, I explored meditation, mindfulness, and yoga. It felt that I was doing it to just say that I was practicing the outer experience, but I was not fully living in the inner experience of moving my energy. One day, an ad had come up on my Instagram. It was for an online class that was a mixture of meditation, yoga, qi gong, and many other energy modalities. I was interested and felt pulled to watch the free masterclass that was available. I watched and felt a connection to the teacher. They started the sales part and I thought in my head, I will buy this course if it is under $300. I was shocked when it was presented as $299. At that moment I got my card extremely quickly because I felt it was meant to be, even though my fear was present. I had never invested in myself. Little did I know that this was just the beginning of continuously investing in myself to energetically align with a future of my own design. This course was the start of me feeling my energy. Looking back, my inner knowing was guiding me down this path, and I am so grateful that it did. The messages from my inner knowing were always guiding me towards serenity; I just needed to stop and listen.

A great way to get started is by utilizing different forms of bodywork to get your body's energy back into alignment. Energy blocks can be preventing you from true abundant health, vitality, and vibrancy. These blocks can be removed with some great energy practitioners. If you feel like you want to try it out on your own you also can imagine light coming in from above you and below to break up this energy. Keep in mind that this energy exploration can take some practice if you are new to playing with your energy.

As I said before, I was a skeptic. I didn't quite understand my energy, nor did I feel it. As I continue to practice, I feel it more strongly. Energy work is not reducible to one method or practice. There is so much to explore, from charka clearings to Reiki to daily energy clearing routines. Even if someone is not intentionally doing energy work on you, they are manipulating your energy when you are with them. One great exercise is to imagine an imaginary bubble around you, protecting you from others' energies. This is extremely important when you are working on clearing your energy systems.

Reiki has had a powerful effect on me. My first encounter with Reiki was as a child when I had intense surgery. I vividly remember waking up in the hospital from a dream where I had fallen and jolted my system back to a conscious state of mind. A nurse was there and asked me what my pain was on a scale of one to ten. I was so out of it that I said "zero" and as soon as she walked out it was as if I was washed in a wave of pain. I started to wail. When the medical staff came back, I said I was at an eleven-pain level. The nurses and doctors gave me so many pain medications, including morphine, and it didn't work. My whole body felt like it was on fire, and I kept crying because it had hurt so badly. I tried to sleep so that I was no longer consciously aware of my pain. My mother had asked the nurses if they had any alternative healing and learned that two nurses practiced Reiki. We were ready to try anything at that point. I still to this day remember the pain lifting off my body. After the session was over, my pain decreased significantly, and I was able to be discharged from the hospital two days earlier than expected.

It was not until I had my health crisis that I felt I would try Reiki again. This time, instead of seeking Reiki, I became a Reiki practitioner myself. Reiki is a hands-on healing Japanese system that affects a person in all dimensions (physically, mentally, emotionally, and spiritually). It uses the idea that an unseen life force moves through us. In Japanese, "rei" means spiritual wisdom, and "ki" means life force energy. Together, these words mean "spiritually guided life force energy." Reiki is a spiritual practice and is not rooted in any religion, nor is it its own religion.

When you get trained in Reiki, you get "attuned" and taught by a Reiki Master Teacher. In the traditional Usui Reiki System, there is Reiki I, where you perform on only yourself. You practice this for about 21 days before getting the next attunement. Reiki II is where you can start to work on others. You practice for about six months before you become a Reiki Master. Reiki III, also known as a Reiki Master, is someone who is attuned to distance healing in addition to the other trainings. A Reiki Master practices for about one year before reaching the final level. Reiki Master Teacher is the top level that you can reach. It is where you can attune others to become practitioners. I have been trained all the way up to Reiki Master Teacher. I was offered my Reiki I attunement and training as a part of one of my mentoring programs. I did not know what would happen, but the experience highly exceeded my expectations. Those attunements themselves changed me forever. I rediscovered the power of Reiki. Now, when I perform Reiki on my clients, I am always amazed at its immense power.

This magnificent healing is not a one-time occurrence, but it is a repeatable process that I see over and over again. I have seen people transcend through this process. It is truly incredible and magnificent to witness transformation, especially with energy work.

There is so much for you to explore. This process isn't about understanding energy; it is about experiencing it. Energy play is not something you do once and never have to do again.

The healing power of each modality amplifies the other. People may say, "I have tried everything to create the health I desire or manifest the reality I want." Well, have you tried to using multiple modalities consistently all at once? Have you been consistent with these modalities? Have you taken radical responsibility for getting the results that you desire? These modalities are not quick fixes; they are lifestyle changes. You are going to change your life through small and consistent actions.

EMBODIMENT
PRACTICE

I invite you to try both methods listed below and use the synergistic nature to deeply connect with your energy body

1. Sit down and meditate for a few minutes, then allow your body to move the way it wants to and try to not let your intellect get in the way. Just allow your body to flow and move in whatever way feels natural You can even ask aloud, "How do I move

my body the way that it wants to?" Or you can ask your body, "How do you want to move?"

2. Allow an energy practitioner, either in person or from a distance, to work on your energy.

BRINGING
THE THREE S'S
TOGETHER

WHEN I FIRST STARTED USING SPIRITUAL EXPLORA-
tion in my practices, I thought some of it was way too
woo-woo before realizing that it connects deeply with me.
I have this rule that if it feels so right yet I can't quite understand it, I don't try to understand. I do things that serve
me and my highest timeline. As I learn more, I do realize
that some of it is not woo-woo, but I am not going to try
to convince your logical mind of the amazing complexi-
ties of what we call science and spirituality. I don't care if
anything makes me look weird anymore because I own it. I
am safe in my beliefs and my faith has become unshakable.
If you are resistant to doing things because they may seem
weird, I encourage you to get out of your comfort zone.
This is a time to explore your relationship to the safety you
feel in life. This awakening is a journey. It is not a destina-

tion but a constant exploration that can change your life. Spirituality has so much to explore. You do not have to believe in one ideology or dogma. You are allowed to go on this adventure and see what unfolds for you.

As children, we used to believe in magic and see the world through this mystical lens. Many of us lose this magnificence in our life. Children still say "Abracadabra" when they wield their invincible wands. I now know the significance of this term and have brought it into my vocabulary. In Hebrew, "Abracadabra" means "As I speak, I create." These words are extremely powerful.

You have the power to change anything and everything if you allow yourself to explore this magic again. This powerful incantation shows us that we have the power in our lives to create magic. You cannot control everything, but you can create anything. This is where the dance between surrender and serenity meets. You have the power to change your life, but you must first surrender to where you are to manifest what you want to create. Remember your innate power to surrender. Are you ready to actualize all that lies within?

Conclusion

Committing to the Vibrancy Journey

I DID NOT START MY JOURNEY TO EMBODYING HEALTH, vibrancy, and vitality until there was no other choice because I was subconsciously refusing to live a full, happy, and healthy life. I was struggling with an attachment to my physical symptoms, my victimization, and a woe-is-me mentality. I was addicted to my brokenness. I realized I was holding on to my pain to prove to others that I was suffering. I was desperately trying to collect the evidence to have someone see me. Throughout this journey, I now understand I have nothing to prove, nothing to hide, and nothing to defend because no one can tell me what I did or did not go through. I am here to tell you that even though you may have gone through incredible pain in your life, it is time to let that pain go because you now have made beautiful commitments to yourself. Just by reading this book, you have shown great strides in the right direction.

Your life is now in your hands. You may have experienced real pain and suffering, but are you a victim? No. You are now an empowered being getting ready to manifest the vibrant and vivacious life you deserve to live. It is now time to be free from the shackles of your previous sufferings and embrace this new autonomous reality. You are breaking out of your own enslavement and choosing what happens to you.

In my journey, I was searching from the outside for someone to hear me so that they could heal me. Eventually, I realized I was just searching for myself to hear me so that I could heal me. To become my own savior, to become my own hero, to become my own healer, to become my own support, was the greatest accomplishment in my life. Are you going to choose to hear yourself, are you going to choose to support yourself, are you going to choose to become the embodiment of health?

You allow others to be free by being free yourself. This is your time to shine. Your mind will be scared of this change; do not blame it. It can be scary to live a whole new life. Are you willing to put your ego aside to live the life you want to live? Are you willing to live in a whole new reality? Then go do it, because I believe in you.

You are a limitless being. The only limits you have are the restrictions you place on yourself. The sky isn't even the end, because there is an entire universe beyond. Once you start to see that you are limitless, magic happens in your life, and it feels extraordinary. Do not let anyone tell you what you cannot do; they are only speaking from the limitations they place on themselves. You are a boundless being with capabilities beyond what your mind can even comprehend.

You can bring anything you want into form because you are a creative being. You might say, "I am not an artist," and I beg to differ. Every second of the day, you create the dance between your mind, body, and soul. You create heartbeats, electric impulses, and breaths without even having to think about it.

Your words are the song you give out to the world. Your actions play into the dance of our world. Your thoughts come into form in your physical reality. If you are reading this book, you have probably limited your creative abilities for far too long. It is time to be the artist of your life. It is time for you to create the masterpiece that you have always dreamed of, and that all starts with your health, vitality, and vibrancy.

When you realize how intricate and exceptional you

are, you start to choose your reality. You are beautifully designed, and you are an absolute work of art. I encourage you to look in the mirror and see yourself as this master-piece.

Not only are you beautiful, you are also beautifully powerful. It is time you change your story to one of reclaiming the health and life that you deserve. You can make astounding progress when you start to believe it, but it is important to note that your actions towards health are essential to your journey. Even when you envision a life fully embodied, you must take action towards that glorious vision. Believing, envisioning, and action are all essential in your embodiment journey.

It is essential that you believe in the vision that you are creating. Your belief is extremely powerful. Believe deep in your soul that this reality is inevitable. It is not a matter of if, but when. Visualize that healthy and happy future over and over again, and it will become your reality. Your visualizations mixed with feelings of joy and gratitude are your biggest superpower. These feelings allow everything to come into form. Remember to do your best not to come from a place of non-belief, that what you desire won't happen. If you take steps every day, then you, with this deep-seated belief, will create a whole new magical reality. This is your magic, and this is your choice. You can create your reality; you just have to choose it. Once you declare it, it is already yours. Believe it and feel it. Believing in yourself is so important. Place trust in yourself that you can figure this out and create the vibrancy you deserve. You are allowed to believe in the unbelievable. You are allowed to believe in yourself through insurmountable odds.

You have the power to change your health, life, and any part of you. Wake up and make every decision towards connecting to your mind, body, and spirit. It is all about the little decisions. Every choice you make matters. It is about your call to the universe. Ask for what you deeply desire and don't accept anything less. We are not defined by what happens to us, but we are defined with what we do with what we are given. Let every situation in your life be the greatest thing that ever happened to you.

Remember that your inner knowing supports you in this venture. It guides you to your highest reality. You have to just stop and listen. You have to stop the distractions and listen to the callings in your heart. Once you can listen and integrate the lessons from your inner knowing, you will be open to receiving more.

Imagine a life where you are completely free to do and be whomever you want to be. Imagine that when you wake up in the morning, your body greets you with gratitude and energy. Imagine being consistently in a state of bliss where your body feels that it is receiving an internal massage. Imagine breathing in and out love; imagine it filling every cell of your being. Imagine being unbound. Imagine being free to do any activity you want without restrictions. Imagine breaking the chains and living a lighter and freer life. Imagine transforming victimhood to artistry of healing, transforming darkness to light, transforming unknowing to clear steps toward embodying true health, and transforming shackles of pain to keys of freedom. You can create this reality by listening to your intuition and using multidimensional transformation codes. Your intuition brought you to this book. You were meant to hear this message.

This moment is your chance for complete transformation. It might be scary because so much in your life will change. So much light will radiate off of you when you become a beacon of love. This is the moment you commit to yourself, when you vow to love yourself from this day forward so that you may be the example for others to reclaim their birthright of radiance. I am so proud of you for choosing you, for choosing to embody health at all levels, for daring to envision a life you deserve, and for doing what it takes to get there. Thank yourself for daring to create this reality for yourself. Believe in yourself, because I sure do.

Now that you have all of these tools, what are you going to do with them? Are you ready to embody true health, happiness, and vitality? Are you ready to integrate these lessons? Are you willing to stay where you are in your health and life or are you ready to transform? Are you ready to be vibrant? The choice is yours.

Acknowledgments

Writing this book has been a healing journey of its own and has brought me profound growth, insights, and wisdom. The adventure of writing this book would have been much harder if I didn't have the immense support and the most incredible people that I have in my life!

First, I would like to thank my parents Christopher and Allison Chapman for giving me the opportunities that they never had for themselves, giving me a safe space to be fully myself, to make my own mistakes, and to lead my own way. I would not be who I am today without the wisdom, support, and encouragement throughout the years.

A big thank you to my sister and brother Olivia and CJ Chapman for always being the rocks in my life, for always giving me a big hug when I need it, and for teaching me what is important is always love.

I have so much gratitude for my friends who have given me strength, support, and love even when things aren't sunshine and rainbows and always being there for me to share joy, laughter, and the adventures of life together! You are my soul tribe; you are the ones that make life worth living.

A huge thank you to all my mentors who shifted my mindset, resourcefulness and who have helped me with everything I have accomplished in this book and beyond with a special thank you to two of my mentors Ivan Rose and Solomon Potter for always believing in me.

I want to thank every single person who has ever come into my life, those who we may have had a deep relationship or have been a messenger of many lessons for me to acquaintances who just said something kind, to the strangers that smiled at me when I needed it the most. Everyone who has come into my life I know you were in it for a reason, and I am grateful to every single one of you.

Of course, I also want to celebrate myself because isn't that what I teach? I want to thank every single part of me, from the parts that did not want to be vulnerable in this way, to the part of me that was excited to share with an open heart. To the little girl within me who gave me the strength to remember who I truly am.

Notes

1. "Vibrant Definition and meaning." Merriam-Webster.com Dictionary, Merriam-Webster, https://www.merriam-webster.com/dictionary/vibrant. Accessed 10 Sep. 2022.

2. Brinkman, J. E., F. Toro, and S. Sharma. "Physiology, Respiratory Drive - StatPearls - NCBI Bookshelf." Physiology, Respiratory Drive - StatPearls - NCBI Bookshelf, June 8, 2022. https://www.ncbi.nlm.nih.gov/books/NBK482414/.

3. Avram, R., G. H. Tison, K. Aschbacher et al. "Real-World Heart Rate Norms in the Health eHeart Study - PMC." PubMed Central (PMC), June 25, 2019. https://www.ncbi.nlm.nih.gov/pmc/articles/PMC6592896/

4. Ralston, Amy, and Kenna Shaw. 2014. "Gene Expression Regulates Cell Differentiation | Learn Science at Scitable." Nature.com. 2014. https://www.nature.com/scitable/topicpage/gene-expression-regulates-cell-differentiation-931/.

5. Gibney, E. R., and C. M. Nolan. "Epigenetics and Gene Expression - Heredity." Nature, May 12, 2010. https://www.nature.com/articles/hdy201054.

6. Mancilla, V. J., N. C. Peeri, T. Silzer, et al "Frontiers | Under-

standing the Interplay Between Health Disparities and Epigenomics." Frontiers, January 1, 2001. https://www.frontiersin.org/articles/10.3389/fgene.2020.00903/full.

7. Sivadas, Athira, and Kendal Broadie. 2020. "How Does My Brain Communicate with My Body?" Frontiers for Young Minds 8 (October).

https://kids.frontiersin.org/articles/10.3389/frym.2020.540970

8. Mateos-Aparicio, P., and A. Rodríguez-Moreno. "Frontiers | The Impact of Studying Brain Plasticity." Frontiers, January 1, 2001. https://www.frontiersin.org/articles/10.3389/fncel.2019.00066/full.

9. About Adult Stem Cell Therapy. "About Adult Stem Cell Therapy." Accessed September 10, 2022. https://www.kumc.edu/research/midwest-stem-cell-therapy-center/stem-cell-information/about-adult-stem-cell-therapy.html.

10. Annunziato, Anthony. 2008. "DNA Packaging: Nucleosomes and Chromatin | Learn Science at Scitable." Nature.com. 2008. https://www.nature.com/scitable/topicpage/dna-packaging-nucleosomes-and-chromatin-310/.

11. Lenoir, M., F. Serre, L. Cantin, and S. H. Ahmed. "Intense Sweetness Surpasses Cocaine Reward - PMC." PubMed Central (PMC), August 1, 2007. https://www.ncbi.nlm.nih.gov/pmc/articles/PMC1931610/.

12. The Role of Functional Food Security in Global Health | ScienceDirect. "The Role of Functional Food Security in Global Health

| ScienceDirect." Accessed September 10, 2022. https://www.sciencedirect.com/book/9780128131480/the-role-of-functional-food-security-in-global-health.

13. Chang, Tammy, Nithin Ravi, Melissa A. Plegue,et al 2016. "Inadequate Hydration, BMI, and Obesity among US Adults: NHANES 2009-2012." Annals of Family Medicine 14 (4): 320–24. https://doi.org/10.1370/afm.1951.

14. Popkin, B. M., K. E. D'Anci, and I. H. Rosenberg. "Water, Hydration and Health - PMC." PubMed Central (PMC). Accessed September 10, 2022. https://www.ncbi.nlm.nih.gov/pmc/articles/PMC2908954/.

15. Ernst, E., E. Pecho, P. Wirz, and T. Saradeth. 1990. "Regular Sauna Bathing and the Incidence of Common Colds." Annals of Medicine 22 (4): 225–27. https://doi.org/10.3109/07853899009148930.

16. Crinnion, Walter. 2007. "Components of Practical Clinical Detox Programs--Sauna as a Therapeutic Tool." Alternative Therapies in Health and Medicine 13 (2): S154-156. https://pubmed.ncbi.nlm.nih.gov/17405694.

17. Crinnion, Walter J. 2011. "Sauna as a Valuable Clinical Tool for Cardiovascular, Autoimmune, Toxicant- Induced and Other Chronic Health Problems." Alternative Medicine Review: A Journal of Clinical Therapeutic 16 (3): 215–25. https://pubmed.ncbi.nlm.nih.gov/21951023/.

18. Belkaid, Y., and T. Hand. "Role of the Microbiota in Immunity and Inflammation - PMC." PubMed Central (PMC). Accessed

September 10, 2022. https://www.ncbi.nlm.nih.gov/pmc/articles/PMC4056765/.

19. Singh, Rasnik K., Hsin-Wen Chang, Di Yan, Kristina M. Lee, et al. 2017. "Influence of Diet on the Gut Microbiome and Implications for Human Health." Journal of Translational Medicine 15 (1). https://translational-medicine.biomedcentral.com/articles/10.1186/s12967-017-1175-y.

20. "Rapid and Unexpected Weight Gain after Fecal Transplant." n.d. ScienceDaily. Accessed September 10, 2022. https://www.sciencedaily.com/releases/2015/02/150204125810.htm.

21. Knight, R. "Rob Knight: How Our Microbes Make Us Who We Are | TED Talk." Rob Knight: How our microbes make us who we are | TED Talk. Accessed September 10, 2022. https://www.ted.com/talks/rob_knight_how_our_microbes_make_us_who_we_are?language=en#t-459258.

22. Satokari, Reetta. 2020. "High Intake of Sugar and the Balance between Pro- and Anti-Inflammatory Gut Bacteria." Nutrients 12 (5): 1348. https://www.ncbi.nlm.nih.gov/pmc/articles/PMC7284805

23. Blum, W. E., S. Zechmeister-Boltenstern, and K. M. Keiblinger. "Does Soil Contribute to the Human Gut Microbiome? - PMC." PubMed Central (PMC), August 23, 2019. https://www.ncbi.nlm.nih.gov/pmc/articles/PMC6780873/.

24. Oschman, J. L., G. Chevalier, and R. Brown. "The Effects of Grounding (Earthing) on Inflammation, the Immune Response, Wound Healing, and Prevention and Treatment of Chronic In-

flammatory and Autoimmune Diseases - PMC." PubMed Central (PMC), March 24, 2015. https://www.ncbi.nlm.nih.gov/pmc/articles/PMC4378297/.

25. Carpenter, Siri. 2012. "That Gut Feeling." Https://Www.apa. org, September 2012. https://www.apa.org/monitor/2012/09/gut-feeling.

26. Larrick, Jasmine W., Andrew R. Mendelsohn, and James W. Larrick. 2021. "Beneficial Gut Microbiome Remodeled during Intermittent Fasting in Humans." Rejuvenation Research 24 (3): 234–37. https://pubmed.ncbi.nlm.nih.gov/34039011/.

27. Liess, M., S. Henz, and N. Shahid. "Modeling the Synergistic Effects of Toxicant Mixtures - Environmental Sciences Europe." SpringerOpen, September 19, 2020. https://enveurope.springeropen.com/articles/10.1186/s12302-020-00394-7.

28. Don Miguel Ruiz. 2008. The Four Agreements and The Four Agreements Companion Book. Amber-Allen Pub.

29. Cascio, C. N., M. B. O'Donnell, F. J. Tinney, M. D. Lieberman, et al "Self-Affirmation Activates Brain Systems Associated with Self-Related Processing and Reward and Is Reinforced by Future Orientation - PMC." PubMed Central (PMC), November 5, 2015. https://www.ncbi.nlm.nih.gov/pmc/articles/PMC4814782/.

30. Kiken, L. G., and N. J. Shook. "Does Mindfulness Attenuate Thoughts Emphasizing Negativity, but Not Positivity? - PMC." PubMed Central (PMC). Accessed September 10, 2022. https://www.ncbi.nlm.nih.gov/pmc/articles/PMC4178287/.

31. Galante, Julieta, Ignacio Galante, Marie-Jet Bekkers, and John Gallacher. 2014. "Effect of Kindness-Based Meditation on Health and Well-Being: A Systematic Review and Meta-Analysis." Journal of Consulting and Clinical Psychology 82 (6): 1101–14. https://pubmed.ncbi.nlm.nih.gov/24979314/.

32. Bai, Z, J Chang, C Chen, P Li, K Yang, and I Chi. 2015. "Investigating the Effect of Transcendental Meditation on Blood Pressure: A Systematic Review and Meta-Analysis." Journal of Human Hypertension 29 (11): 653–62. https://pubmed.ncbi.nlm.nih.gov/25673114/.

33. Hilton, Lara, Susanne Hempel, Brett A. Ewing, et al. 2016. "Mindfulness Meditation for Chronic Pain: Systematic Review and Meta-Analysis." Annals of Behavioral Medicine 51 (2): 199–213. https://www.ncbi.nlm.nih.gov/pmc/articles/PMC5368208/.

34. Cahn, B. R., M. S. Goodman, et al. "Frontiers | Yoga, Meditation and Mind-Body Health: Increased BDNF, Cortisol Awakening Response, and Altered Inflammatory Marker Expression after a 3-Month Yoga and Meditation Retreat." Frontiers, January 1, 2001.https://www.frontiersin.org/articles/10.3389/fnhum.2017.00315/full#:~:text=In%20line%20with%20a%20hypothesized,was%20reduced%20after%20the%20retreat

35. Dahl, Cortland J., Antoine Lutz, and Richard J. Davidson. 2015. "Reconstructing and Deconstructing the Self: Cognitive Mechanisms in Meditation Practice." Trends in Cognitive Sciences 19 (9): 515–23.https://pubmed.ncbi.nlm.nih.gov/26231761/),

36. Hölzel, B. K., J. Carmody, M. Vangel, C. Congleton, S. M. Yer-

ramsetti, T. Gard, and S. W. Lazar. "Mindfulness Practice Leads to Increases in Regional Brain Gray Matter Density - PMC." PubMed Central (PMC), November 10, 2010. https://www.ncbi.nlm.nih.gov/pmc/articles/PMC3004979/.

37. Brewer, J. A., P. D. Worhunsky, J. R. Gray, Y.-Y. Tang, J. Weber, and H. Kober. 2011. "Meditation Experience Is Associated with Differences in Default Mode Network Activity and Connectivity." Proceedings of the National Academy of Sciences 108 (50): 20254–59.https://www.pnas.org/doi/abs/10.1073/pnas.1112029108

38. Braboszcz, C., B. R. Cahn, J. Levy, M. Fernandez, and A. Delorme. "Increased Gamma Brainwave Amplitude Compared to Control in Three Different Meditation Traditions - PMC." PubMed Central (PMC), January 24, 2017.https://www.ncbi.nlm.nih.gov/pmc/articles/PMC5261734/).

39. Radin, Dean, Gail Hayssen, Masaru Emoto, and Takashige Kizu. 2006. "Double-Blind Test of the Effects of Distant Intention on Water Crystal Formation." EXPLORE 2 (5): 408–11. https://pubmed.ncbi.nlm.nih.gov/16979104/, Durkin, Patrick. 2017. "Dr. Masaru Emoto and Water Consciousness." Structured Water Superstore. March 23, 2017. https://thewellnessenterprise.com/emoto/.

40. "The Eyes Have It: Mutual Gaze Potentially a Vital Component in Social Interactions." n.d. Eurek Alert! Accessed September 10, 2022. https://www.eurekalert.org/news-releases/663914.

41. Tolle, Eckhart. The Power of Now. New World Library, 2004.

Additional Support

If you are ready for additional guidance in your journey, I am more than ready to be your sister in co-creating ultimate vibrancy. If you feel drawn to these teachings and are ready to have more support in implementing them, I invite you to reach out.

EMAIL ME:

cassidyamberchapman@gmail.com

FOLLOW ME ON:

Instagram: @cassidyamberchapman
Facebook: @cassidyamberchapman

VISIT:

www.thevibrancycodes.com